D0874075

National Self-Determination
in Postcolonial Africa

National Self-Determination
in Postcolonial Africa

Ralph Benyamin Neuberger

Lynne Rienner Publishers, Inc.
Boulder, Colorado

Published in the United States of America in 1986 by
Lynne Rienner Publishers, Inc.
948 North Street, Boulder, Colorado 80302

Library of Congress Cataloging-in-Publication Data
Neuberger, Benyamin, 1943-
    National self-determination in postcolonial Africa.

    Bibliography: p.
    1. Africa—Politics and government—1960–
2. Self-determination, National.   I. Title.
DT30.5.N48   1986   320.96   85-25628
ISBN 0-931477-46-8

Distributed outside of North and South America and Japan
by Frances Pinter (Publishers) Ltd, 25 Floral Street,
London WC2E 9DS England. UK ISBN: 0-86187-96-6

Printed and bound in the United States of America

PREFACE

During a panel on "National Self-Determination in Africa—Reconsidered" at the 1984 African Studies Association Annual Convention in Los Angeles, a heated debate developed between the Ethiopian, Eritrean and Somali participants on the definition and meaning of the principle of national self-determination. The issue—one of life and death for the participants—focused on the ideological rationale of the wars in the Horn of Africa. The need for a theoretical and comparative perspective to deepen the understanding of the African controversies on national self-determination was evident. This book was written in order to fill this gap in the literature on post-colonial Africa.

This book was written while I was on a sabbatical leave at the University of Pennsylvania. I wish to thank the Penn-Israel Foundation and its chairman, Professor Norman Oler, and the Israeli Open University and its president, Professor Abraham Ginzburg, for the financial support which made my stay in Philadelphia possible. I wish also to thank Professors Alvin Rubinstein, Donald Smith and Harvey Glickman for their friendship and encouragement.

Professor John Ayoade of Ibadan University (Nigeria) read the manuscript and made important suggestions. Ms. Patty Rosenblatt deserves thanks for her perceptive and helpful editorial comments. Thanks also to Ms. Lynne Rienner who encouraged me to expand a paper given at the ASA Annual Convention into this book-length study.

Benyamin Neuberger

ABBREVIATIONS

AAPC	All African Peoples' Conference
ABAKO	Alliance des Bakongo
AEF	Afrique Equatoriale Française (French Equatorial African Federation)
AG	Action Group
ALM	Afar Liberation Movement
ANC	African National Congress
AOF	Afrique Occidentale Française (French West African Federation)
CONAKAT	Confédération des Associations Tribales du Katanga
CPNC	Cameroons People's National Convention
CUT	Comité du l'Unité Togolaise
DOM	Départment d'outre mer
ELF	Eritrean Liberation Front
EPLF	Eritrean People's Liberation Front
EPRP	Ethiopian People's Revolutionary Party
ERIC	Ethiopian Revolutionary Information Center
FLEC	Frente para Libertacao do Enclave de Cabinda
FLN	Front de Libération Nationale
FNLA	Frente Nacional de Libertação de Angola
FRELIMO	Frente de Libertação de Mozambique
GAR	General Assembly Resolution
KADU	Kenya African Democratic Union
KANU	Kenya African National Union
MOLISAN	Mouvement Libération Sanwi
MPLA	Movimento Popular de Libertação de Angola
NCNC	National Council of Nigeria and the Cameroons
NFD	Northern Frontier District
NIBMAR	No Independence Before Majority Rule

OAU	Organization of African Unity
OLF	Oromo Liberation Front
PAFMECA	Pan African Movement of East and Central Africa
PAIGC	Partido Africano da Independência da Guiné e Cabo Verde
POLISARIO	Frente Popular Para la Liberación de Saguia el Hamra y Rio de Oro
SADR	Sahara Arab Democratic Republic
SALF	Somali Abbo Liberation Front
SSLF	Southern Sudan Liberation Front
SWAPO	South West African People's Organization
TFAI	Territoire Français d'Afars et d'Issas (French Territory of the Afars and the Issas)
TOLIMO	Togoland Liberation Movement
TOM	Territoire d'outre mer
TPLF	Tigre People's Liberation Front
UC	Union Camerounaise
UDI	Unilateral Declaration of Independence
UNITA	União Nacional para a Independência Total de Angola
UPC	Union Populaire Camerounaise
WSLF	Western Somali Liberation Front

CONTENTS

INTRODUCTION

The principle of national self-determination has been haunting the world since the French Revolution. There may be no other term in modern political discourse which is used with more emotion and passion. Recent history has known many wars fueled by conflicting interpretations of self-determination. Woodrow Wilson thought that implementation of the principle of self-determination would lead to a better world—a world without wars and "safe for democracy." His secretary of state, Robert Lansing, had his doubts. He suspected the concept of self-determination to be "loaded with dynamite"[1] and capable of causing even more bloodshed because it "will raise hopes which can never be realized."[2]

In both colonial and postcolonial Africa bitter struggles and bloody wars have been fought in the name of national self-determination. A close look at the use of the concept in Africa and a comparison of conflicting African interpretations of the principle of national self-determination with similar controversies elsewhere will reveal important insights about African patterns of nation building. An analysis of the concept of national self-determination, of its use and misuse in Africa, is crucial to the understanding of postindependence Africa. Only an in-depth analysis of the concept of national self-determination and its component parts will lead us to a true understanding of the dilemmas involved in the secessionist wars of Katanga, Biafra, Eritrea, and the Southern Sudan. It will enable us to better our grasp of the periodic crises and tensions between Cameroun and Nigeria, Morocco and Algeria, Ghana and Togo, or Libya and Chad. It will provide us with neglected tools for understanding the irredenta of "Greater Somalia" and "Greater Morocco." It will shed light on a host of other conflicts in postcolonial Africa—from the separatist efforts of Buganda, Barotse, and Sanwi in the 1950s, to the war in Cabinda and the secession of Mayotte in the 1970s. It will also provide a framework which will help us understand the tensions, crises, and wars that we are likely to see in Africa in the decade to come.

The basic approach of this book is interdisciplinary, combining comparative politics with philosophical, historical, and legal approaches. Studies on national self-determination to date have been monopolized largely by jurists. Michael Walzer observed in his study on the concept of a "just war" that "the lawyers have constructed a paper world, which fails at crucial points to correspond to the world the rest of us live in."[3] The same is true for the study of national self-determination. Without diminishing the importance of some legal studies on the subject, the controversies over the principle of national self-determination are too serious to leave them solely to the lawyers.

This book deals with the intellectual roots of the principle of national self-determination, with the basic difference between nationalist and liberal-democratic interpretations of national self-determination, with conflicting definitions of the "self," with the various goals of self-determination, and with the mechanisms and timing of "determination." It analyzes the connection between national self-determination and the right of secession, as well as the question of whether different perceptions of colonialism are relevant to the study of some of the dilemmas involved. The crucial questions of the optimal size of states, the viability of small states, the dangers of "balkanization," and the contradictions between national self-determination and other international norms and principles are also discussed. The final topic is the double standard which has accompanied the principle of self-determination since the French Revolution.

1

INTELLECTUAL ORIGINS

Self-Determination is not a mere phrase. It is an imperative principle of action which statesmen will henceforth ignore at their peril.

Woodrow Wilson, 1918[1]

Among the ideas which dominate political life today, that of national self-determination, occupies not the least important place. Among the peoples whose aspirations are guided by it, it has proved itself of a sort which moves mountains.

Carlisle A. MaCartney, 1934[2]

The term self-determination is used more frequently and with more passion than any other term in contemporary international relations . . . it has also the distinction of being one of the most confused expressions in international relations.

W. Ofuatey-Kodjoe, 1977[3]

The old nationalism and the new nationalism have given millions a chance of greater dignity in the collective enjoyment of the territories in which they live. We cannot believe that these benefits are completely outweighed by the sad stories of wars, massacres, atrocities and torture.

Peter Calvert, 1976[4]

The first precursors of the right of self-determination can be traced to the late Middle Ages and the early Renaissance when Marsilius of Padua talked about legitimate government as based on the consent of the governed and Dante raised the issue of autonomy for cultural groups. In the sixteenth century, the French king, Franz I, objected to a transfer of territory to Spain's Charles V with the argument that you cannot make deals about cities and provinces without their *"consentement exprés."*[5] Legal scholars and Christ-

3

ian philosophers prepared the ground for the democratic ideas of the seventeenth and eighteenth centuries by establishing the right to resist tyrannical authority. The seventeenth century international jurist Hugo Grotius had talked already about the right of resistance and the right of secession ("*ius resistendi ac secessionis*") for oppressed peoples.

The development of the principle of national self-determination was accelerated by the revolutionary and democratic ideas of the seventeenth and eighteenth centuries. Ultimately the principle of self-determination is linked to ideas about natural rights, the rights of man, the sovereignty of the people, the social contract, government by consent of the governed, and the right of revolution against oppressive regimes. To understand the intellectual roots of Wilson's national self-determination and Lenin's principle of nationalities, we have to go back to Locke, Rousseau, and Jefferson and to the revolutions of 1688, 1776, and 1789. The American and French revolutions are important watersheds. Prior to these, although the theory of the right of peoples to determine their government was well known for centuries, the actual political practice was the right of *rulers* to determine the sovereignty and form of government of "their" territories but never the right of *peoples* to self-determination. Two other important sources for the development of the principle of self-determination were Kant's idea of the will as autonomous and free from external constraints and romantic notions glorifying natural spontaneity, diversity, and solidarity.[6] National self-determination is basically a collectivization of Kant's idea of the autonomous will of individuals. It is the people's will which must be free. Thus a people has the right to determine its life and institutions—a right to self-determination.

Toward the end of the eighteenth century, radicals and liberals (and even some conservatives) in Europe resented the fact that people were traded like chattel among the ruling dynasties and that only brute force decided the people's fate. Regarding the transfer of Corsica to France, Burke commented that a "nationality was disposed of without its consent like the trees on an estate."[7] The cry for national self-determination arose as a protest against national oppression, against empires which were "prisons of nations," and against "artificial" borders which cut across "natural" ethnocultural nations. Behind the principle of national self-determination was the vision of a new order in which political and ethnic borders would coincide and in which a system based on natural nation-states would assure international peace and stability.

In the nineteenth century, national liberation movements fought their way to power in Greece and Latin America. Canada and Australia became sovereign. German and Italian nationalists succeeded in unifying their countries, and Poles, Irish, Czechs, Hungarians, and Norwegians formed national movements and struggled for independence. The pursuit of happiness was now sought for peoples, and everywhere the cry was heard, "a state for every nation and all the nation in one state." In 1865, the principle of national self-determination was specifically mentioned for the first time when the First Socialist International demanded national self-determination for the Polish people.

The principle of national self-determination as a moral issue dominated much of Europe's politics during the latter half of the nineteenth century. In World War I, Woodrow Wilson led the United States into the war in order to make the world safe for democracy and national self-determination, while Lenin led the Soviet Union out of the war proclaiming the principle of nationalities as a new guiding principle for a socialist world order. Later, the principle of national self-determination was universalized and legalized. While in the post-World War I era people talked only about the *principle* of national self-determination, after World War II, international conventions established the *right* of peoples to national self-determination. Today, many international jurists agree that national self-determination is no longer solely a moral demand and a political principle, but in many circumstances, a legal right recognized by international law. Indeed, national self-determination appears after 1945 in all important documents relating to the organization of the international community. The United Nations (UN) Charter speaks about "the principle of equal rights and of self-determination of peoples,"[8] while the International Covenant on Human Rights says that "all peoples and all nations shall have the right of self-determination."[9] The ambiguity and ambivalence contained in the principle of self-determination are best shown by the fact that opposing sides in many international conflicts often justify their positions by resorting to it. They can do so because there is no agreement on what is "national," what is the "self," and what "determination" means. The principle has thus acquired almost universal acceptance, but the interpretations to which it is subjected continue to be widely divergent.

In Africa, the principle of national self-determination was first invoked after World War I. The Pan-African Congress which convened in 1919 in Paris coined the slogan "Africa for Africans," and in the early 1920s, Egyptian nationalists demanded independence in the name of national self-determination. But in general, until World War II, the principle of national self-determination was regarded as important for the evolution of a new European order but irrelevant to the colonies of Africa and Asia. Things changed in 1945 when the UN Charter proclaimed the right of *all* peoples to national self-determination. The fifth Pan-African Congress in 1945 in Manchester affirmed "the right of all people to control their own destiny" and demanded "autonomy and independence" for black Africa.[10] In all of Africa in the late 1940s and the 1950s, the call for national self-determination and liberation from colonial rule was heard. The liberal, democratic, and national ideas of Europe had penetrated the African continent and were now mobilized against the European colonial powers. The peoples of Asia and Africa who demanded independence and freedom were now "claiming against the West the right to imitate the West."[11] The ideas of national self-determination, that peoples cannot be traded, and that every people has the right to rule itself were proclaimed in the Atlantic Charter to be the core values of the Allies in World War II. This time, as different from World War I, the application of the principle could not be confined to Europe. The Africans demanded their share and got their share.

Initially, the application of the principle of national self-determination in Africa after World War II posed no particular problem—as long as nationalism was essentially defined as anticolonialism. The general acceptance of the right to self-determination vis-à-vis the colonial power was not yet burdened by the knowledge of the dilemmas contained in implementing that right. The following quotations are representative for the era of decolonization:

> The right of self-determination is God-given and no man or nation is chosen by God to determine the destiny of others.[12]

> The right of free determination can at no moment be considered as subversive . . . it is the natural right of peoples be they large or small, it is the right of liberty.[13]

Before we proceed to demonstrate that later in postcolonial Africa things looked less "natural" and more complex, and before we begin to dissect the principle into its components, let us be aware that there are *principles* of national self-determination, not *one* principle which applies to all situations. We have to differentiate between "external self-determination" ("the right of every people to choose the sovereignty under which they live") and "internal self-determination" ("the right of every people to select its own form of government").[14] External self-determination may also mean the right of a nominally independent state to true independence (e.g., the right of the communist states of Eastern Europe to follow an independent foreign policy rather than operate as satellites of the Soviet Union), while internal national self-determination may also refer to minority regimes, regional autonomy schemes, or federalism within an established state. That means that one may talk about two varieties of external self-determination—true independence for a state (e.g., for Poland) and internationally recognized independence for a people (e.g., for the Basques). In addition, there would be three varieties of internal self-determination—democracy in a homogeneous state (e.g., Holland), autonomy or federalism for a distinct people within a democratic state (e.g., the Québecquois in Canada), or autonomy/federalism for a distinct group within a nondemocratic system (e.g., the Georgians in the Soviet Union). The distinction between states and nations (or peoples, nationalities, ethnic groups, or any other distinct population) with regard to national self-determination is a crucial one. While there are 1500 nations in the ethnocultural sense on the globe—all *potential* candidates for external sovereignty or internal autonomy—there are only 150 sovereign states and only about 15 states in which state and nation completely overlap.

Sometimes external and internal self-determination are completely interwoven and cannot be separated. For example, the choice given to Puerto Rico in the 1960s involved both external self-determination (independence or no independence) and internal self-determination (statehood or associated status). The choice given to Hawaii was also a combination of both varieties of self-determination, because the alternative offered was incorporation into the United States (the external sovereign) as a state (the internal autonomy). Another important distinction is between "individual self-determination," which involves the protection of the individual's basic freedoms and the right of political participation, and "collective self-determination," which relates to the right of groups and peoples.[15] Socialists and nationalists may talk about "economic self-determination."[16] Socialists will talk about internal economic self-determination—the emancipation of the working-class from exploitation by the capitalist owners of the means of production—while nationalists may talk about external economic self-determination. An example of the concept of external economic self-determination is the clause in the International Covenant on Economic, Social and Cultural Rights which says that "the right of people to self-determination shall also include permanent sovereignty over their natural wealth and resources."[17] The concepts of internal or external economic self-determination have more far-reaching implications than "political self-determination," which aims only to establish external sovereignty or an internal constitutional framework without insisting on socioeconomic changes. Also different from political self-determination is "cultural self-determination"—the right to teach and study in one's own language, to develop an autonomous culture, and to resist assimilation by a dominant power.[18] In the twentieth century Third World, there is also a crucial distinction between "colonial (or better, anticolonial) self-determination," which is the liberation of Asian or African peoples in a colony from European colonial rule, and secessionist self-determination, which represents a people's aspiration to break out of the postcolonial state and achieve liberation for one Afro-Asian people from rule by another Afro-Asian people.

We may simplify all these distinctions by establishing a dichotomy between "grand self-determination," whose object is true internationally recognized sovereignty, and "small self-determination," which deals with the internal structure and politics of the state. Grand self-determination is more external, collective, political, anticolonial, or secessionist, while small self-determination is more internal, individual, economic, and cultural. We should keep in mind that reality is more complex and also includes internal political self-determination and external economic self-determination.

In postcolonial Africa, all these concepts have their relevance. External self-determination, as an effort of nominally independent states to achieve true independence, appears in Africa in the form of ideologies and policies which aim to reduce dependency, fight neocolonialism, and increase self-reliance. External self-determination, in order to achieve independent statehood, was the aim of anticolonial nationalism and of secessionists in Katanga, Southern Sudan, Biafra, and Eritrea. Some of the ethnic separatists had to content themselves with internal self-determination in the form of a federal state (in Nigeria) or regional autonomy (in the Sudan). As elsewhere, in Africa, too, the issues of internal and external self-determination are sometimes linked. In the Congo (Zaire) in the early 1960s, four different currents were struggling for prominence—unitarism, federalism, confederalism, and separatism. While Lumumba's unitarists and Tshombe's separatists fought over the issue of external self-determination, the confederalists and federalists strove for compromise by internal self-determination. In Nigeria, too, the 1960s were characterized by a clash of unitarists, federalists, regionalists, confederalists, and separatists. Calls for separatist (external) self-determination in the North in July 1966 were a result of the dissolution of the Federation and the adoption of unitarism by the Ironsi government. The Biafran bid for independence was also a result of the abandonment of the confederal Aburi scheme and the abolition of the Four Region Federation by the Gowon government. In the Sudan and Eritrea, also, the struggle was not only between separatists and unitarists but also involved federalists and regional autonomists. When the British Cameroons had to decide in 1961 whether to join Nigeria or Cameroun, only external self-determination was involved. The struggle in Kenya in the early 1960s between the federal Kenya African Democratic Union (KADU) and the unitarist Kenya African National Union (KANU) dealt only with internal self-determination. But in Zaire, Nigeria, Sudan, and Ethiopia the issues of internal and external self-determination were inseparably linked.

The debate in Africa between supporters and opponents of Western democracy is in essence a debate on the relative importance of individual versus collective self-determination. Calls for external economic self-determination have been echoed in Africa by radical leaders like Kwame Nkrumah, Sekou Touré, Julius Nyerere, Samora Machel, and Augustino Neto, all of whom called to break the economic dependency on foreign governments and foreign companies by advocating policies of nationalization, diversification of crops, changing sources of aid and foreign-trade partners, militant anti-imperialism, and by presenting a mystique of self-reliance. While external economic self-determination was propagated by radical nationalists, internal economic self-determination was supported by revolutionaries. The military leaders of Ethiopia, for example, regarded the liquidation of the rural aristocracy as a precondition for economic self-determination of the peasant masses. Sometimes internal economic self-determination has contained a racial dimension. For example, Idi Amin called the expropriation and expulsion of the Asian minority in Uganda a "war of economic liberation" because it broke the economic power of the Asian middle-class and supposedly freed the Africans from Asian economic domination. The expulsion was popular in Uganda for a time as it was seen as economic self-determination by the African masses.

Africa has also known cultural self-determination both in the external and internal sense. External cultural self-determination is essentially cultural decolonization—a turn, or return, to African history, literature, names, dresses, and languages. The aim of external cultural self-determination is a return to roots and authenticity in order to break the degrading dominance of European cultures, languages, and behavior patterns. Cultural decolonization is a natural by-product of nationalism, which always wants the nation to be distinct, unique, and equal in value to other nations. Cultural self-determination in the internal sense relates to aspirations of African ethnic groups for schooling in their language, for the recognition of their language in government and administration, or for religious liberty. Examples are the demands of the non-Amharas in Haile Selassie's Ethiopia or of the African Southerners in pre-1972 Sudan.

Colonial self-determination has been the most common form of self-determination in post-World War II Africa. It has meant that the population of a colony, a "*Staatsnation*" which usually has had no ethnocultural unity but has been arbitrarily delimited by the colonial partition, gained independence. Colonial self-determination was intercontinental and directed against European rulers. Ethnic or secessionist self-determination, however, is very much in dispute, supported by disaffected ethnic groups and widely condemned by the political establishment of Africa—the Organization of African Unity (OAU) and the majority of the ruling governments. The ethnic and secessionist bid for self-determination frequently involved a "*Kulturnation*" (e.g., the Somalis in the Ogaden) or a territory with at least one ethnocultural core (e.g., the Ibos in Biafra).[19] Ethnocultural self-determination closely resembles the European variety of national self-determination, a product of nationalism which in Antony Smith's words "remains a doctrine of history and destiny of the *nation*, an entity opposed to other important modern collectivities like the sect, state, race or class."[20]

Anticolonial self-determination is indeed hardly national self-determination as it is colony-based and not nation-based. Anticolonial self-determination is, from a postcolonial perspective, statist and conservative, while ethnic and secessionist self-determination is revisionist and wants to tear down the current state system. Ethnic-secessionist self-determination is different from anticolonial self-determination in the sense that it is intracontinental and inter-African and does not involve Europe and the Europeans.

2

DEMOCRATIC DETERMINATION OR NATIONAL DETERMINISM?

Free institutions are next to impossible in a country made up of different nationalities.
John Stuart Mill, 1861[1]

There is clearly very much in the demand for national self-determination which is absolutely consonant with true democracy. Its victories have usually, in fact, been victories of liberty over unjustifiable tyranny.
Carlisle A. MaCartney, 1934[2]

Independence has been valued and alien rule resented by many more peoples than have aspired to democracy and individual freedom.
John Plamenatz, 1960[3]

Self-determination must be perceived as an international human right.
Yoram Dinstein, 1980[4]

Today most people would rather be governed poorly by their ethnic brethren than well by aliens, occupiers and colonizers . . . indeed to be ruled by ethnic strangers is perceived as worse than oppressive.
Josef Rothschild, 1981[5]

Among politicians and scholars there is no consensus as to whether national self-determination means national government (a *French* government in France), democratic self-government (an *elected* government in France), or a combination of the two (an elected and French government in France). National government need not be democratic (France under Marshall Pétain), while democratic government need not be national (Brittany is part of democratic France, but it is not ruled by a national Breton government).

The democratic school defines national self-determination as government by consent of the governed and not as national government per se. The nation according to the democratic school is defined by territory and not according to any ethnocultural criteria. National self-determination was perceived in essence as the principle which allowed "people of a given territory to determine their own government."[6] National self-determination was equal to democratic self-government. Hans Kohn argued that the American concept of national self-determination is based on democratic rather than purely national claims. Its major ingredients—the "inalienable rights of man," "consent of the governed," and "no taxation without representation"—were more democratic than national.[7] In 1776, there wasn't any distinct American nation to fight for national statehood. The Americans fought for democratic rights by demanding the people's right to self-determination. Only after self-determination was achieved did they become a nation.

Elie Kedourie, too, regards the Anglo-Saxon definition of national self-determination as inherently democratic. Kedourie thinks the post-World War I Versailles system in Europe was based on a "misunderstanding" between the democratic version of self-determination of Woodrow Wilson and Lloyd George and the East European variety which stressed "national" rather than "self-determination."[8] For the Anglo-Saxons, dictatorial government is government foreign to the people—whether the rulers are real foreigners or local usurpers of power. For that reason, Wilson's Fourteen Points talked about granting the peoples of Austria-Hungary the "freest opportunity for autonomous development" and not about an automatic establishment of nation-states by the nations of the former Empire.[9]

The liberal-democratic concept of national self-determination demands respect for basic human rights, protection of minorities, equality for all individuals and groups, free elections, and the right to participate in government. This purely democratic concept of self-determination was pursued in the 1940s and 1950s by many of Africa's Francophone leaders. Leopold Senghor, Félix Houphouët-Boigny, and even Sekou Touré and Modibo Keita believed for a while that because of the nationalist excesses of Fascists and Nazis and the growing interdependence of the world, national independence or "separatism" was an outmoded concept. They sought self-determination in the full democratization of the French Empire and in their participation as full partners in the political life of France—"une et indivisible." They demanded local self-government, equality before the law, and "one man one vote" for the Africans of "la France d'outre-mer." France, in a sense, succeeded in assimilating the Francophone African elite and convincing it to think French. But the democratic school of self-determination failed in the end in Africa. While the African elite was ready to transcend national self-determination for democratic self-determination, the same was not true for France itself. To follow consistently the policy of assimilation and democratization would have led to the transformation of the French nation-state to a multinational and multiracial state in which the French could have become a minority. These prospects led the French to retreat gradually from the vision of one Franco-African Empire. John Plamenatz observed that "the French could have enlarged their own freedom and given freedom to the peoples subject to them and still have drawn them as willing partners into a close political union with themselves. They do not seem to have done it."[10] The British never gave their African subjects any illusions about one united democratic empire. The French promised one democratic French Union but never intended seriously to keep their word. Events of the late 1950s and early 1960s revealed Africa's disillusionment with the purely democratic road to self-determination.

The national school of self-determination defines the achievement of independence as the goal of national self-determination. National self-determination is perceived as fulfilled as long as the citizens of the nation are ruled by their "kith and kin." In fact, most states in the world are independent but not free in the democratic sense. Many nationalists have cut the principle of national self-determination from its democratic roots. They are willing to accept "less autonomy with more flag."[11] Hans Kohn conceded that these nationalists fought for liberty, but "the liberty worshipped was not so much individual freedom but freedom from foreign government."[12] National self-determination according to the nationalists' point of view is compatible with dictatorship as long as it is national. Polish and Hungarian nationalists who fought for national self-determination before World War I saw nothing wrong in establishing national dictatorships after gaining independence. For German nationalists, freedom consisted in national sovereignty and not Western democracy. When the Sudeten Germans in 1938 overwhelmingly supported a return to the Reich in the name of national self-determination, they in fact opted to leave democratic Czechoslovakia, where they had all the democratic rights, in order to join Hitler's Nazi Germany. For them, national self-determination meant to be ruled by fellow Germans rather than to live in a democratic state.

In Africa, the discrepancy between democratic and national approaches to self-determination is clearly visible. Independence from colonial rule is certainly regarded as a true fulfillment of national self-determination, but by the yardstick of democratic self-determination, Africa in the 1980s is not free. When Touré defied France in 1958, he said that the people of Guinea preferred freedom in poverty to servitude in plenty. The overwhelming majority of the people of Guinea followed his lead in opting for independence and in rejecting continued French rule within the French Community. But in retrospect, the vote was not for democratic freedom but for national independence. Touré's bloody dictatorship (1958–1984) can hardly be reconciled with any definition of democratic freedom. Thus, like the Poles after

World War I, the people of Guinea exchanged not servitude for freedom, but colonial servitude for independent servitude. Ronen's observation about present day Africa that "an authoritarian ruler from among 'us,' even a dictator like Idi Amin, may provide a greater sense of freedom than a democratic foreign ruler" refers to the same phenomenon.[13]

The shift from national self-determination as a formula for democracy to national self-determination as a prescription for a nondemocratic nation-state can proceed even further. It can start from a proposition that the people have the right to decide in which state they will live, even if that state is internally dictatorial (e.g., the decision by plebiscite of the Saar Germans in 1935 to join Nazi Germany), and it can reach a point where a national elite "determines" to what nation-state a specific people belongs, without ever asking the people involved (e.g., the 1940 declaration by Nazi Germany that all the people of Alsace-Lorraine were Germans and part and parcel of "Greater Germany"). This completes a full circle from an arbitrary state-system determined by kings and armies, via national self-determination and a state-system based on the people's will, to arbitrary "national determinism" by self-proclaimed national elites.

In Africa, an example of this shift can be found in the Moroccan attitude towards the Western Sahara. In the early 1960s, Morocco still supported the right of the Saharans to decide by self-determination the future of the Spanish colony (hoping that they would opt to unite with the "motherland"). By 1975, when the aspirations for independence among the Saharwi became known, the Moroccan position shifted to national determinism—to opposition to any referendum because of a belief in "One Moroccan Nation" which had determined that the Western Sahara was part of it. A similar national determinism does not allow the Ethiopians to accept self-determination in the Ogaden, Eritrea, or Tigre. The same applies for the Comorians with regard to Mayotte, for the Angolans with regard to Cabinda, for the Zairians with regard to Shaba (Katanga), and for the Sudanese with regard to the Southern Sudan.

The African preference for national self-determination as opposed to democratic self-determination is in one important sense different from the Eastern European examples between the World Wars. In Poland, Hungary, and Rumania, national self-determination was regarded as implemented as long as the nation-states which were dominated by one ethnocultural nation were independent and led by Poles, Magyars, or Rumanians. In Africa the independent states are, to a large extent, plural societies, and most frequently there is no common national identity and no dominant ethnocultural core comparable to the Eastern European cases. That may mean that after independence was achieved, the populations in the African states felt themselves to have national self-determination only in the sense that "national" means black-African as opposed to white-European. The overthrow of the authoritarian colonial governments was perceived by most Africans as genuine liberation. These emotions were even stronger where there was a European settler population as in Kenya, Rhodesia, Angola, and Mozambique (the same is true for Zanzibar where an Arab oligarchy ruled until 1964). Nevertheless, while there certainly exists a vague, racial, pan-African solidarity and identity, it is certainly too diffuse and weak to be called truly national. While ethnic groups which dominated (e.g., Hausa-Fulani, Kikuyu, Amhara, Lango, Bemba, Shona) or shared in African governments (e.g., Yoruba, Kamba, Tigrineans, Acholi, Bakongo) may very well have felt themselves to have achieved national independence and self-determination, that sentiment may not have been shared by Oromos and Eritrean Muslims in Ethiopia, the Turkana and Somalis of Kenya, the Lunda and Bayeke of Zaire, the Toubou (before 1979) and Sara (after 1979) of Chad, the Ndebele of Zimbabwe, the Touareg of Mali, or the Toucouleur of Mauritania. For many African ethnic groups, national self-determination may be perceived as liberation from European colonial rule, but not as the establishment of a government belonging to "us." For them, national self-determination in the sense of having "our" government did not materialize. Furthermore, the collapse of parliamentary democracy in Africa in the 1960s has indicated that democratic self-determination, in the Wilsonian sense, was also not realized.

The confusion as to what constitutes national self-determination has its roots in the past association between democracy and nationalism, for both had in common the goals of popular sovereignty and participation. Later on, the conservative opponents of democracy and socialism discovered the potential power of nondemocratic nationalism for undermining mass support for democrats and socialists through "populistic" appeals. For example, in 1848, liberals and socialists fought alongside others in Germany for German unification. Their fiercest enemy was the oppressive kingdom of Prussia. Later in the 1860s and 1870s, Bismarck adopted the goal of German unification and achieved it by "blood and iron." That enabled the conservative and monarchical forces to do away with the liberal and socialist threat for more than half a century. Thus, the two notions of what constitutes national self-determination first diverged with the split between democratic and antidemocratic nationalism in the midnineteenth century.

There are very few cases in European history where a people opted for a national dictatorship in preference to a foreign democracy (as in the case of the Saar Germans in 1935 and the Sudeten Germans in 1938) or where a people voted to prefer a foreign democracy to a national authoritarian regime (as in the case of the Tessin Italians who several times rejected the temptation to join Italy and preferred to remain "*liberi e svizzeri*" as an ethnocultural minority).[14] In Africa, both cases are unknown because colonial rule was not democratic and very few people in the 1940s and 1950s knew that postcolonial Africa would not be democratic. Shortly after independence, the African states abandoned Western democracy. Thus, there was never a real choice between national self-determination and democratic self-determination.

In addition to the two definitions of national self-determination which emphasize either democratic self-government *or* national independence, there is a third way to define national self-determination by combining the aspects of democracy, rejection of foreign rule, and national independence. E. H. Carr, for instance, sees the democratic and national aspects as interlocking: "If every man's right is recognized to be consulted about the affairs of the political unit to which he belongs, he may be assumed to have an equal right to be consulted about the form and the extent of the unit."[15] In recent history, those who fought for national self-determination very often fought for both national independence and democracy. The Atlantic Charter of 1941 also linked both aspects of self-determination by establishing the right of peoples to have a say in the type of sovereignty under which they want to live and by stressing their right to have a democratic form of government. Plamenatz goes so far as to argue that the whole notion of foreign rule as illegitimate has its roots in an era when "democracy and individual freedom became common ideas."[16]

The question may be raised of why democracy alone does not appear to be sufficient for those who want freedom? Why do they aspire to have both national and democratic self-determination? The answer is that in a stable and functioning democracy, the minority must have the feeling that it may sometime become a majority. In a multinational and heavily polarized democracy, the minority nation feels it has no chance ever to rule the whole country or to participate in government. The Irish felt that way in nineteenth century Britain, and therefore, they fought for secession, although as individuals they had all the democratic rights in the United Kingdom. For a minority nation to live in a nation-state which is firmly identified with a dominant nation and where the dominant nation may exploit its numerical preponderance and disregard aspirations of the minority, the democratic state may not be much different than a tyranny. For that very reason, John Stuart Mill regarded national self-determination as a precondition for political freedom. He supported the nation-state to achieve democracy and supported democracy to achieve the nation-state.[17]

In Africa, the anticolonial nationalism of the 1940s and 1950s combined national and democratic aspects very well. It was national in the sense that it was directed against foreign European rule. It is hypothetically possible that even if all the democratic rights would have been granted to the Kenyan Africans or to the Algerian Arabs, we still might have seen a struggle for national self-determination and for severence of the constitutional links to the colonial power. But anticolonial nationalism was also a call for democratic self-determination, as it was embedded in the liberal democratic tradition. Its slogans were basically democratic—"government by consent of the governed," "one man, one vote," "equal rights," and "equal pay for equal work." Early liberal anticolonial nationalism in Egypt (in the early 1920s) and in Tunisia and Morocco (in the early 1940s) definitely linked the goals of independence and the establishment of constitutional democracy. The same was true for the fifth Pan-African Congress (Manchester, 1945) which called for democratic freedoms and for African independence. In the 1940s and 1950s Kwame Nkrumah, Jomo Kenyatta, Nnamdi Azikiwe, Kenneth Kaunda, and Julius Nyerere frequently quoted the Atlantic Charter which combined the call for national and democratic self-determination. In numerous UN resolutions which dealt with the colonial question, the national and democratic dimensions were linked. The UN resolutions in the 1950s, 1960s, and 1970s on Belgian Ruanda-Urundi, Spanish Equatorial Guinea and the Western Sahara, French Djibouti, Portuguese Angola and Mozambique, Rhodesia, and Namibia combined the demand for decolonization with the insistence on freedom of speech, abolition of press censorship, the cessation of arbitrary arrest, and the right to form political parties and hold free elections.

Only by the 1960s and 1970s did it become clear that harsh realities—a backward economy, scarce resources, demographic pressures, the rise of unrealistic expectations, and endemic ethnic strife—were forcing the African leaders to abandon the liberal-democratic ingredients of anticolonial national self-determination. In postcolonial wars and conflicts, the principle of national self-determination has become a tool in the intellectual arsenal of the parties, but it no longer resembles the liberal self-determination of the 1940s and 1950s. While the African states which gained independence in the early 1960s experimented with democracy for a few years, those becoming independent in the 1970s usually perceived national self-determination from the beginning as national government and not as democratic government. Only very rarely in postcolonial Africa were the linkages between democracy and nationalism and between human rights and independence reestablished. One such rare occasion was when Nyerere granted recognition to Biafra declaring that "there is something basically unsound in the UN insistence on self-determination as a human right and as a means for independence when this is coupled with relative unconcern over and inability to safeguard individual rights once independence is achieved."[18]

In Africa in the 1970s and 1980s, the dominant concept is external anticolonial self-determination and not internal democratic self-determination. The struggle for self-determination is regarded as terminated once independence is achieved. There is much opposition to interference in national affairs for the sake of internal self-determination. There are two exceptions to the rule that postcolonial African self-determination does not address itself to the internal structure of the state. The exceptions are the white-minority regimes in Rhodesia (1965–1979) and South Africa. Externally, they were independent, whether recognized by the UN (South Africa), or not (Rhodesia). As a matter of fact, Ian Smith, in his Unilateral Declaration of Independence (UDI), based his claims on the rights of a colony to national self-determination. In African eyes, national self-determination in these cases did not mean simply external independence. It also entailed majority rule. In Rhodesia, the Africans stuck to the principle of NIBMAR (no independence before majority rule). Their position on South Africa is similar. The Africans' demands for majority rule were, even in these cases, more demands for rule by the black majority as a collective unit than for majority rule in the Western parliamentary sense. Ali Mazrui introduced the term "pigmentational self-determination" to explain the demand to replace white minority rule with black majority rule. For similar reasons, support for India was strong in Africa when it invaded and annexed Portuguese Goa. In African eyes, it was a conflict between white Portuguese and nonwhite Indians, although the similarly nonwhite Goanese were widely reported to oppose annexation by India. "Anti-European self-determination" may be a more exact term than "pigmentational self-determination" because the pigmentational logic was not widely followed in Africa when it came to take a stand on Northern Arab rule over Southern black Africans in the Sudan. The same was true with regard to Arab rule in Zanzibar (until its overthrow in 1964) and Moorish domination of the Toucouleur, Wolof and Sarakollé in Mauritania. While there was an African consensus to achieve national self-determination for the Africans in the European-ruled colonies and in South Africa, the demands for national self-determination for black African peoples under Arab domination enjoyed less legitimacy.

3

WHAT IS THE "SELF"?

On the surface it seems reasonable: let the people decide. It was in fact ridiculous because the people cannot decide until somebody decides who are the people.

Sir Ivor Jennings, 1963[1]

Nationalism pretends to supply a criterion for the determination of the unit of population proper to enjoy a government exclusively its own.

Elie Kedourie, 1960[2]

Our aim has been to create genuine nations from the sprawling artifacts the colonialists carved out.

Kenneth Kaunda, 1969[3]

Tous ceux qui se ressemblent, se rassemblent.

Abbé Fulbert Youlou, 1960[4]

The solidarity that a nationalist desires is based on the possession of the land, not any land but the historic land.

Antony Smith, 1979[5]

National self-determination assumes the presence of a "national self," but what is a national self? The UN Charter declares that "all peoples have the right to national self-determination," but who is to decide what a "people" is and who are "all" the peoples? One may say a nation, or a people, has to be a "distinct self," but who is going to determine what is distinct? Were the Americans in 1776 a distinct people from the British? Are the Germans distinct from the Austrians? There are no easy answers, but we can agree that "the determination of which 'self' is entitled to determine 'what,' and 'how' remains the central question."[6] The problem with the concept of national self-determination has much to do with the wide dissensus as to what constitutes a true national self. Conflicting views of this question have led to many bitter struggles and bloody wars.

The British who opposed Irish independence recognized only one British national self, while the Irish nationalists regarded themselves as a separate nation. Lincoln believed in the unity of one American nation, while the southerners identified as a southern nation. Gandhi's Indian nation included Hindus and Muslims, while Jinnah insisted that the Muslims are a separate nation with a right to a state of their own. The conflicts in Central Europe in the 1930s and after World War II in Cyprus, Vietnam, India/Pakistan, Palestine, Lebanon, Kurdistan, Ireland, and Tibet all had something to do with different definitions of the national self.[7]

The emergence of a national self occurs—at least in the formative stages—through a process of differentiation from an opposing group. The formation of an American nation was linked with opposition to the British. The concept of a Pakistani nation does not make any sense without its differentiating stand against the Hindu-dominated Indian nation, and Kurdish identity can only be defined by opposing it to Arab-Iraqui, Turkish, or Iranian nationhood. Smith defines nationalism by three basic characteristics— "definition of given populations as nation," "struggle against foreign rule," and the "aspiration for political independence."[8] Thus, also according to Smith, the definition of the nation is intimately tied to the "struggle against foreign rule." By deciding who is foreign, the nationalists decide also what is the national self.

In Africa, the problem of the proper self to possess the right of national self-determination is alive and well. Even in colonial times, the issue was disputed by colonialists and nationalists. Until World War II, the colonies were regarded as integral or organic parts of the imperial whole, and thus, any application of the principle of national self-determination was rejected as illegitimate. The French even called their colonial empire "France overseas" and declared it to be "one and indivisible." They followed a policy of "assimilation" and talked about "black Frenchmen." Well into the late 1950s, Africans served in the French National Assembly, Council of the Republic, and the Cabinet. With regard to Algeria, feelings that it was an integral part of France were especially strong. Even the liberal Prime Minister Pierre Mendès-France declared the Algerian "*départements*" to be as French as France. For the French governor general of Algeria in 1955, Jacques Soustelle, Algeria and all its inhabitants were "an integral part of France" like the Provence and Brittany.[9] Both the leftist Mendès-France and the rightist Soustelle regarded any armed opposition to the concept of "*Algérie française*" to be a challenge to the territorial integrity of France. The Fifth Republic Constitution of 1958 still declared Algeria to be an integral part of the French Republic. In the same way, the Portuguese regarded Guinea-Bissau, Cape Verde,

Sao Tome and Principe, Angola, and Mozambique as overseas provinces of metropolitan Portugal and refused cooperation with the UN on their decolonization. The leader of the 1974 Portuguese Revolution, Antonio de Spinola, realized the basic fallacy of the colonial philosophy by saying that "it is not *national* unity that is at stake, but *imperial* unity."[10] Spain also saw Rio Muni, Fernando Poo, Rio de Oro, Sakiet al Hamra, and Ifni as overseas provinces. Typical of this imperial view is a Spanish declaration in 1958 that "Spain possesses no non-self-governing territories since the territories subject to its sovereignty in Africa are provinces of Spain."[11] King Baodouin of Belgium declared a few years before the Belgian Congo (Zaire) became independent that the Congo is "integrally" linked with Belgium and that this will ensure "the perpetuity of a genuine Belgo-Congolese community."[12]

The view that there is one Euro-African national self was also shared in the 1940s and 1950s by many African leaders—especially in the French colonies. Among those in the post-World War II period who defined national self-determination as the democratization of one French-African Union, Community, or Federation we find not only Leopold Senghor, Aimé Césaire, Félix Houphouët-Boigny, Gaston Monnerville, and Gabriel d'Arboussier, but even Ferhat Abbas and Sekou Touré.[13]

In the era of decolonization, the decision what constituted the self was often much more important than the 'free' determination. This was the case in post-World War I Europe and was no different in Africa towards the late 1950s. The division of the British Cameroons into two selves for the purpose of the UN supervised plebiscite in 1961 brought about a pro-Nigerian decision in the North (146,269 to 97,659) and a verdict for unification with former French Cameroun in the South (233,571 to 97,741). If the whole territory had counted as one self, the *whole* territory would have joined Cameroun. In British Togoland, the refusal to partition the territory into ethnolinguistic selves (as a UN Visiting Mission had suggested) for the 1956 vote on the future of the territory forced the Ewe-populated south into an unwanted union with Ghana. While an overwhelming 81 percent voted in northern British Togoland for union with Ghana, only 23 percent did so in the Ewe-south. Because the whole territory was counted as one self, by a 58 percent majority, the whole territory was joined to Ghana. In the Djibouti plebiscites of the 1960s and 1970s, a separate count in the southern Somali *cercles* of Djibouti and Ali Sabieh and in the northern Danakil *cercles* of Dikhil, Obock, and Tadjoura might have produced a partition, with the south going to Somalia and the north opting for continued French rule, unification with Ethiopia, or independence. The fact that all parties concerned insisted the Djibouti was one self brought about independence as a compromise between the conflicting claims of Ethiopia and Somalia. Another interesting case is that of the Comoro Islands, which consist of Grande Comoro, Moheli, Anjouan, and Mayotte. The French decided to conduct the 1974 plebiscite on independence separately for each island ("*consultations des populations*") and not for the Comoros as one whole ("*consultations de la population*"). The Comoros were thus split into four selves for the sake of self-determination. Although 95 percent of the population as a whole voted for independence, the majority on Mayotte (8,783 to 5,110) opted to remain French. Thus, Mayotte was separated from the other islands and remained a "*territoire d'outre-mer*" (TOM). The Comoros declared independence in 1975 and denounced the violation of their "territorial integrity" by secessionist Mayotte.

The Colony Turned State

In Europe, we know that different systems of foreign rule led ethnic-cultural clusters to split into different nationalities. Czechs and Slovaks, Serbs and Croats, and Letts and Lithuanians owe their distinct national identities to different forms of foreign rule. In these cases, differential foreign rule lasted for centuries and thus became a basis for separate nationhood. With the exception of the Portuguese colonies, colonialism was in power in most parts of Africa for less than a century, and it is questionable whether this short episode in African history constitutes enough history for the crystallization of a national self. With some exceptions (Somalia, Swaziland, Lesotho), the European colonies in Africa contained ethnically heterogeneous populations, and thus, their claims to be national selves for the sake of national self-determination were different from the claims made by the Poles, Czechs, Slovaks, Croats, Serbs, and the Irish.

The national self in Africa is most frequently defined as the former colony in its colonial boundaries. An overwhelming majority of the African political establishment affirms the importance and even decisiveness of colonial history in the building of African nations. Anti-colonial nationalism, in most cases, was a struggle for the independence of colonies as territorial units within their colonial boundaries (some of which were finally decided only in the 1950s and 1960s, as in the cases of French West Africa, French Equatorial Africa, Spanish Equatorial Guinea, and the Western Sahara). The governments of Nigeria, Zaire, Sudan, Zambia, Kenya, the Comoros, Angola, Mali, Niger, and the Ivory Coast fought secession by sanctifying the territorial integrity of the postcolonial state within its colonial boundaries. The African establishment would agree with the following statement by Mali's former president Modibo Keita:

> We must take Africa as it is, and we must renounce any territorial claims, if we do not wish to introduce what we might call black imperialism in Af-

rica . . . African unity demands of each one of us complete respect for the legacy that we have received from the colonial system, that is to say: maintenance of the present frontiers of our respective states . . .[14]

African leaders would agree that in many independent states, there are not yet national selves in the ethnocultural sense, but they will insist that the current states are the means to achieve true nationhood. According to Touré, "in Africa it is the state which constructs the nation."[15] The OAU position truly reflects this "statist nationalism" of most governments. In its Cairo Declaration of 1964, the OAU declared that "the borders of the African states on the day of independence constituted a tangible reality," and because of that, "the member states pledge themselves to respect the borders existing on their achievement of independence."[16] Since its foundation in 1963, the OAU as an organization (although not all governments in all cases) never supported a secessionist movement. The strong commitment to independence and territorial integrity within colonial boundaries also explains the nearly total opposition to any notion of partition of South Africa and to the independence of the Transkei, Ciskei, Venda, and Bophutatswana. The "*bantustans*" or ethnic homelands, are not regarded as legitimate national selves for self-determination in South Africa and Namibia not only because they reflect a divide and rule strategy of the ruling whites, but also because the legitimization of the Transkei, Kwazulu, or Ovambostan will make it difficult to deny legitimacy to ethnic self-determination in Iboland, Luo Country, or Buganda. René Johannet said about nationhood that "the cause of the statue is not the marble but the artist."[17] In Africa, the colony (and the independent successor state) is the "artist" which has to build a nation (the "statue") in spite of the ethnocultural mix (the "marble"). The established position among the African political elite is that the potential nation, although short of being a national self in the classical sense, is the relevant unit for national self-determination. If this African interpretation of national self-determination had prevailed after World War I, the Irish, Letts, Estonians, Lithuanians, Poles, and Czechs would not have been granted independence, because anticolonial self-determination rejects the liberal-nationalist dictum "a state for every nation and all the nation in one state."

The insistence that the African state within its colonial boundaries is the appropriate unit for national self-determination is reflected in the semantics of postcolonial nationalism. European colonialism called the ethnocultural groups in Africa "tribes," a concept with racist connotations of primitiveness. In fact, there is no objective reason to call the few hundred thousand Basques a nation, and the ten million Ibos, who possess a well-defined territory, a language, and a culture, a tribe. The notion that the Europeans form nations and the Africans tribes was simply a reflection of colonial racism which became a moral rationale for colonial rule. Enlightened public opinion could accept colonial rule of tribes and yet be faithful to the Wilsonian principle of self-determination of nations. It is striking that many African leaders continue to talk about tribes in spite of the colonialist-racist connotation of the word. The reason may simply be that it is also psychologically and intellectually easier for them to deny national self-determination to tribes associated with "an atavistic force impeding the growth of national solidarity" than to nations who—according to the Atlantic and UN Charters, democratic liberalism, nationalism, and Marxism-Leninism—should be accorded the right to national self-determination.[18]

Semantic denationalization in order to deny the right of national self-determination and secession is a well-known strategy. After World War I, a Czechoslovak nation was invented in Czechoslovakia in order to counter separatist tendencies among the Slovaks. In Turkey, the Kurds are called "Mountain Turks"; in Bulgaria, the Macedonians are called "Bulgarians"; and in Soviet-ruled Bessarabia, the Rumanians are called "Moldavians." All this was done in order to delegitimize Slovak and Kurdish separatism and Rumanian irredentism.

In Nigeria, the central government defended the denial of self-determination to the Biafrans on the grounds that they are not a nation and thus have no right to national self-determination. The only national self in the eyes of the Gowon government was the whole of Nigeria. The denationalization of the Ibos reflected a real ideological dilemma for the Nigerian leaders who, before 1967, always regarded the major Nigerian ethnic groups, and certainly the Ibos, Yorubas, and Hausas, as nations and not as mere tribes. Since it is difficult to deny the right of secession to nations, the Ibos were stripped of their status as a nation in 1967, and Biafran separatism was declared tribalist.

Likewise, all Ethiopian governments, whether the "*ancien régime*" or the post-1974 revolutionary government, have denied the existence of one Somali nation. They acknowledge only the existence of different tribes who have historically little in common.[19] The whole idea of Greater Somalia as a state for the whole Somali nation has been dismissed as expansionism of the Somali state. Kenya also declared that "there is no such homogeneous entity in Northern Kenya as 'the Somali,'" but a host of different "clans and sections" which are completely "different."[20] The Kenyan government declared that the Somalis in the Eastern Region are simply "Kenya Africans," as are the Kikuyu, Luo, or Kamba.[21] The Kenyans thus not only reject the notion that there is a pan-Somali national self but deny also that the Somalis in Kenya constitute a nationality. The Kenyans officially declared pan-Somalism to be a tribal doctrine.

With regard to Eritrea, too, the Ethiopians deny any notion that there is an Eritrean nation and that the war for secession is a national struggle for self-determination. The Eritrean war is seen as a "foreign inspired seces-sionist attempt" against which Ethiopia has a right to self-defense.[22] The Ethiopians emphasize that there is no Eritrean nation because Eritrea con-tains a dozen ethnocultural groups. Yet, at the same time, both Haile Selassie and Mengistu talked about one Ethiopian nation, which is certainly even more heterogeneous than Eritrea. For Mengistu Haile Mariam's regime, which proclaimed Marxism-Leninism as state ideology, to concede the exis-tence of nations within Ethiopia would be very embarrassing because, ac-cording to the Soviet model, nations have the right to have their own repub-lics and even have the constitutional right to secede. For that reason, the Dergue leaders talk about nationalities which are not full-fledged nations and thus may have only the right for limited regional autonomy. The denial that Ibos, Somalis, Eritreans, Katangese, Southern Sudanese, and Oromos are nations and as such entitled to national self-determination is designed to strengthen the current state-system and the notion that within the colonial boundaries, only Nigeria, Kenya, Ethiopia, or Zaire have the right of self-determination. Some African leaders (e.g., Nyerere, Touré, Haile Selassie, Ironsi) went a step further and prohibited public mention of any tribes, hop-ing thus to do away once and for all with the danger that a tribal (or national) self would reassert its identity and demand self-determination.

The colonial self is not always opposed to the ethnocultural self with regard to self-determination. A few states may regard themselves as true nation-states of one ethnocultural nation (e.g., Swaziland, Lesotho, Bots-wana, Somalia), although in all these cases, there are irredentist aspirations to unite with "brothers and sisters" across the border. Sometimes ethnocul-tural unity is claimed, although it is based on fictions and myths. When Nigeria's foreign minister during the Biafran War claimed that the unity of Nigeria was based on "continuous miscegnation for more than a thousand years,"[23] or when Haile Selassie talked about the "cultural unity" of Ethiopia,[24] what they did was to try by sheer invention to give the statist self an ethnocultural content.

Some other colonial states identify themselves or are identified by others as representing an ethnocultural nation. In the Sudan, the pan-Arabists, the Muslim Brotherhood, and the Ansar and Khatmiyya sects see a Muslim-Arab state. The Northern Sudanese Ghaffar freely admits that the "*Northerners* because in the majority and with better prospects of taking over as successors of the British defined self-determination for the *entire Sudan* as one entity."[25] Thus, in effect, the North implemented self-determination not only for the North to govern itself, but also for the North to rule the South. We may call that "other-determination" rather than self-determination. Many in the African South saw the North-South relationship in the same way, and for that very reason, they fought for secession between 1955 and 1972 and again in the 1980s.

Imperial Ethiopia was based on a Christian-Amhara core and for that reason instituted a policy of Amharization in the school system, administration, and Church and a policy of discrimination against the large Muslim population. Most observers tend to agree that the revolutionary government did not radically undermine the identification of Ethiopia with the Amhara core. Afar nationalists regard Djibouti as an Afar state and a potential base for a larger "Danakilia," while Somali nationalists regard Djibouti as a Somali territory to be united with Somalia. These do not represent demands for ethnocultural self-determination in the sense that the Sudanese Arabs, the Amhara, or the Djibouti Afar want to have independence for their ethnic homelands. In all these cases, an ethnocultural group aims to dominate politically and culturally the whole colonial self which became the postcolonial state.

Support for self-determination within colonial boundaries has been widespread both in the UN and the OAU. Nevertheless, there are exceptions to this rule too. Ruanda-Urundi was one political-administrative unit under German (1890–1918) and Belgian (1918–1962) colonial rule. Still, in 1962 almost all African states supported a UN resolution which stated that "the best future for Ruanda-Burundi lies in the evolution of a single united and composite state."[26] Liberia's Angie Brooks, representing the African position on this issue, called any notion of partition a step towards the balkanization of Africa.[27] Nevertheless, the hostility between Tutsi-ruled Burundi and Ruanda where the Hutu gained political power in 1959 proved too intense, and finally, the UN succumbed to the ethnic realities and the wishes of the populations involved and approved the partition of the colonial self into two independent states—Rwanda and Burundi. Similarly, the division of the British Cameroons between Nigeria and Cameroun was generally accepted, although in this case, one colonial self was divided between two neighboring states. There was also no objection raised to the unification of two former colonial units as was the case in British Somaliland and Italian Somalia, the British Southern Cameroons and French Cameroun, the British Northern Cameroons and Nigera, British Togoland and Ghana, and finally Zanzibar and Tanganyika. In these cases, new selves were created by the combination of two colonial units. There was also no opposition to the transfer of the Spanish protectorates of Northern and Southern Morocco, the Ifni enclave, and internationalized Tangier to full Moroccan jurisdiction. Even the military conquest by Benin of the tiny Portuguese enclave of Sao Joao Batista de Ajuda was accepted as legitimate.

There is a strong tendency in the Third World not to recognize the right of national self-determination within colonial boundaries of colonial enclaves like Gibraltar, Goa, Macao, and Hong Kong; and in Africa, of entities like Ifni, Tangier, Cabinda, Ceuta, and Melilla. It is interesting that anticolonial self-determination within colonial boundaries is not in dispute in equally small islands and archipelagos like the Comoros, Cape Verde Islands, Sao Tome and Principe, Mauritius and Réunion. Towards the continental islands the attitude is harsher and less liberal.

Usually, emphasis on the colonial territory as the relevant self for self-determination is associated with statist nationalism which wants to preserve the status quo, deny any legitimacy to secession, and oppose boundary revisions. Sometimes, however, secessionists fight for national self-determination for the population of a territory which was a colonial self. Eritrean separatism offers such a special case because it aims to undo Eritrea's incorporation into Ethiopia accomplished during decolonization and to restore the former Italian colony in its colonial boundaries as an independent state.[28] For the Eritrean nationalists, life under Italian (1890–1941) and British (1941–1952) colonial rule constitutes a common historical experience which provided the Eritreans with a newly defined separate identity—a "sense of common fate and incipient nationhood."[29] Eritrea should never have been annexed by Ethiopia but should have been granted the right of national self-determination and become independent. They say, furthermore, that in the Treaty of Wuchale (1889) and again in the agreement following the battle of Adowa (1896), Ethiopia renounced all claims to Eritrea and thus recognized it as a distinct colonial entity. The Eritrean case is an intriguing one because although secessionism is not based on religious, ethnocultural, or historic unity, the secessionist war which started in 1962 is the longest and one of the bloodiest in Africa's postcolonial history. Eritreans are indeed no "*Kulturvolk*" but a "*Staatsvolk*" like the populations in most independent African states. The Eritreans are composed of at least eight major linguistic groups (Tigrinya, Tigre, Afar, Saho, Bilen, Beja, Baria, Kunama) and even more ethnocultural groups (e.g., the Tigre-speakers don't identify as one group). The language gaps are sometimes fairly wide, as some of the languages are Semitic and others Hamitic and Nilotic. In addition, the population is divided between Muslims and Christians and between agriculturalists and pastoralists. Reflecting these divisions is the fact that the secessionist guerilla movements don't succeed in unifying with one another and frequently clash. Nevertheless, all the movements speak of an "Eritrean people" and all want independence for the territory as a whole. Whatever bonds exist between the Eritreans reflect "the fact of living together within frontiers which were now defined as those of a separate entity."[30] In the Eritrean case, too, there are some nationalists who try by fabricating myths and propagating fictions to give the colonial self an ethnocultural content. Thus, the Eritrean Liberation Front (ELF) talked frequently about the Eritreans as an "Arab nation" both in order to gain support from the Arab world and to legitimize the claim for national self-determination (the concept of an Eritrean nation may be in dispute, but nobody denies the existence of an Arab nation—the fact that the Eritreans are not Arabs is a different story).

Another interesting case is the Western Sahara, a former Spanish "overseas province," which was partitioned between Morocco and Mauritania in 1976 and later on annexed *in toto* by Morocco. The *Frente Popular Para la Liberación de Saguia el Hamra y Rio de Oro* (POLISARIO) guerillas have fought the Moroccan occupation force for almost a decade and did so in the name of national self-determination for Sakiet al Hamra and Rio de Oro within their "historical boundaries."[31] Thus, the Spanish colonial boundaries have been declared historical, and in this way, the Western Sahara as a proper unit for national self-determination has become legitimized, and its borders sanctified. While the Eritrean Liberation Front (ELF) and Eritrean People's Liberation Front (EPLF) were never accorded recognition by the OAU and most African governments, POLISARIO succeeded in 1981 in achieving diplomatic recognition for the Sahara Arab Democratic Republic (SADR) by the majority of Africa's states and by the OAU itself in 1984. In both Eritrea and the Western Sahara, the guerilla movements have strong popular support for national self-determination and for independence for the former colonial self. Nevertheless, there are two crucial differences which may explain the relative success of POLISARIO and failure of the ELF/EPLF to gain international legitimacy: Eritrea was unified with Ethiopia in 1952 by a decision of the UN General Assembly, while Morocco's annexation of the Western Sahara was achieved by the Green March of 1976 and military occupation later on. The takeover of Eritrea by Ethiopia in 1952, and even the abolition of Eritrea's federal status *within* Ethiopia in 1962, occurred before the foundation of the OAU and the establishment of the sanctity of colonial boundaries, while the Moroccan unification with the Western Sahara occurred more than a decade later. In the cases of Eritrea and the Western Sahara, the national self fighting for self-determination was definitely a colonial self.

In numerous other cases, revisionists of all sorts, whether separatists, irredentists, regionalists, or pan-Africanists, supported their claims at least partially by referring to some colonial self. It is thus quite misleading to identify all revisionists with a total and principled opposition to any colonial border, treaty, agreement, or declaration. That is certainly not the case with the Eritreans and Saharwi. To a certain degree, Somali, Katangese, Biafran, Southern Sudanese, Baganda, Sanwi, Lozi, Cabindan, and Mahorais revisionism also referred to *some* colonial self.

The successful Kamerun movement and the unsuccessful Togoland movement both sought to substitute the pre-World War I colonial self for the post-World War I colonial self.[32] The disagreement between Togo and Ghana and between Cameroun and Nigeria was about which colonial self should be the proper unit for national self-determination and independence. In French Cameroun in the 1940s, the radical nationalists of the *Union*

Populaire Camerounaise (UPC) already supported the reestablishment of German Kamerun in its pre-World War I boundaries. They were joined in these demands in the late 1950s by the conservative *Union Camerounaise* (UC), led by Ahmadu Ahidjo. In the British West Cameroons, various groups and movements supported different colonial selves for self-determination. There were those who supported a united Kamerun within the German colonial boundaries, those who supported independence for the West Cameroons within the 1918–1960 colonial boundaries, and others who supported the integration of the British Cameroons with Nigeria, with which the Northern Cameroon (1918–1960) and the Southern Cameroon (1918–1954) were administratively amalgamated for most of the post-World War I period. In 1961 the Nothern Cameroon indeed opted for integration with Nigeria, while the Southern Cameroon voted for unification with French Cameroun. The different determinations of Northern and Southern Cameroon may have had something to do with their different colonial status in the 1950s. While Northern Cameroon was completely integrated into Nigeria's Northern Region between 1974 and 1961, the Southern Cameroon became a separate region from 1954 to 1961. In this way, Southern Cameroon was a colonial self, which was more differentiated from Nigeria than Northern Cameroon. That means that in the 1950s, in both the French Cameroun and the British Cameroons, there were several colonial selves competing to become proper units for self-determination. Camerounian nationalists have not abandoned the hope that North Cameroon—now a part of Nigeria—would return to the Cameroun Republic, which reunited the former French Cameroun and British Southern Cameroon. During Ahidjo's presidency, Cameroun annually observed a day of mourning to commemorate the day when Northern Cameroon was lost to Nigeria.[33] According to Ahidjo, the Camerounians were attempting "de retrouver leurs frontières du passé."[34] But the nostalgia is not for the precolonial past. It is for the Kamerun of the German colonial period.

In British Togoland (now a part of Ghana), for decades there were Ewe-led parties and movements (e.g., the Deutsch Togobund in the 1930s, the Togoland Union in the 1940s, the Togoland Congress in the 1950s) which demanded reunification with French Togo (now Togo Republic). They wanted to create a united Togo in what was German Togoland between 1890 and 1918. In the 1970s the Togoland Liberation Movement (TOLIMO) vowed to continue the fight for Togolese union. In the Togo Republic, the *Comité de l'Unité Togolaise* (CUT), the ruling party in the early 1960s, strongly advocated Togolese unification. The present ruler of Togo, Col. Gnassingbe Eyadema, also makes repeated demands for a return to the colonial border of 1890. Eyadema, a non-Ewe "Northerner" has thus adopted the demands of earlier Ewe nationalists (e.g., Togo's first president, Sylvanus Olpympio) for the reestablishment of a united Togo.[35]

The Somalis also emphasize that they were in fact unified under Italian colonial rule from 1935 to 1941, when Italy created one Somali province in Italian East Africa. They further mention that they remained *de facto* united under one British administration from 1941 to 1948 (and partially until 1954).[36] A major argument of the Kenyan Somalis against their inclusion in an independent Kenya was that during the colonial period, the Somali-inhabited Northern Frontier District (NFD) was administered as a Closed District separate from the rest of Kenya. The Somali nationalists have demanded the incorporation of the whole of Djibouti and the Kenyan NFD in a Greater Somalia, although in both cases major parts of these colonial units (55 percent of the NFD and 75 percent of Djibouti) are not inhabited by Somalis. The Kenyans have hinted that they may also lay claims to Somali territory by calling Somali Jubaland (which was transferred from British Kenya to Italian Somalia in 1924) "Eastern Kenya."[37] The insistence that the Afar-inhabited northern part of Djibouti and the western portion of the NFD, populated by the Orma, Boran, Rendille, Gabbra, Gelubba, Samburu, and Sakuye, will be part of reunified Somalia reveals that the Greater Somalia nationalists' policies are also based on the notion that colonial political units (Djibouti) and administrative entitied (NFD) are indivisible and proper units for self-determination.

Secessionists in the 1950s and 1960s in both Eastern and Northern Nigeria asserted that the different methods of colonial rule in the North and South of Nigeria made it impossible to regard Nigerian colonial history as one. Ojukwu, who led the secession against the "colonial federation," at the same time defended colonial political divisions when he argued that because Biafra had been ruled as a single political unit it was entitled to national self-determination. Antony Enahoro, Nigeria's minister of information during the Biafran War, countered that "the act of union which created Nigeria also created Eastern Nigeria (Biafra) and there was Nigeria long before there was an entity known as Eastern Nigeria."[38] "Long before" refers to twenty-five years of colonial history (Nigeria was established in 1914 and the Eastern Region in 1939). In essence, the debate was whether Nigeria as a whole or Biafra was the more authentic *colonial* self for independent statehood.

Southern Sudanese nationalists devoted much energy to proving that in colonial times the British administration regarded the Northern Sudan and the Southern Sudan as distinct political units.[39] Southern Sudanese Bona Malwal lucidly summed up all the colonial-historical arguments that demonstrated that North and South do not belong together: A Closed District Order separated the South from the North and Northerners needed a special permit to enter the South. Northern merchants needed, by the Permission of Trade Order, a special license to trade in the South. The South had a separate colonial administration, a distinct colonial army (the Equatoria

Corps), and a different educational system. According to Malwal, in the 1930s the British even entertained ideas of unifying the Southern Sudan with British East Africa. "Southerners did not know the North and Northerners did not know the South" in the colonial period.[40]

Baganda and Sanwi separatists emphasized not only their precolonial independence but also their autonomy under colonial rule—an autonomy which the postindependence governments of Uganda and Ivory Coast were determined to destroy. Lozi separatism in Zambia in the early 1960s was based on the distinct status of Barotse in colonial Northern Rhodesia. The traditionalist separatists argued that according to the 1890 Barotse Treaty between the British South Africa Company and Paramount Chief Lewanika, Barotseland was a distinct protectorate with its own native government, and as such, it was entitled to independence from the rest of Northern Rhodesia.[41] The Katanga secessionists also stressed colonial history to justify their cause. They claimed that Katanga was not initially part of the Congo Free State and was administered as a separate unit by the *Compagnie du Katanga* (1891–1900) and the *Comité Spécial du Katanga* (1900–1910). They claimed that even after its incorporation into the Congo, Katanga was not administered from the center (Boma until 1925 and Leopoldville later) and that until 1933 it had an autonomous vice governor. Sometimes the African separatists even referred to the separatist tradition of Katanga, although this tradition was colonial and based on the European settlers in Katanga who thought that Katanga could develop into an autonomous "White Dominion." Katanga's declaration of independence on July 11, 1960 in the name of the right of peoples to national self-determination was not limited to the Lunda heartland but covered the whole colonial province of Katanga.

The separatists on Mayotte Island who wanted to secede from the Comoros emphasized, in addition to religious and ethnic differences, that between 1841 and 1893 Mayotte was under a separate colonial administration.[42] In 1958, Mayotte became a separate *département d'outre-mer* (DOM). In the early 1960s the French again decided to grant each of the four Comoro Islands a large measure of autonomy, including a separate elected assembly and an island government (*conseil de préfecture*). In the early 1970s, the French developed each island as a separate colonial self, although officially the Comoros remained one colonial entity until the declaration of the Comoro Republic. Nevertheless, by 1972, Pierre Messmer, the French minister in charge of overseas departments and territories (DOM and TOM), declared that "nothing would be done without a referendum in which each island would be called upon to decide its own future."[43]

The secessionists in the Cabinda enclave who are presently fighting for separation from Angola also stress different colonial history as justification for secession. They point out that Cabinda was a distinct colonial protectorate and that only as recently as 1955 did it become a district in the Angolan overseas province and subordinate to the governor general of Angola. The Cabindan nationalists organized in FLEC (*Frente para Libertacao do Enclave de Cabinda*) argue that this transfer to Angola was a blatant breach of the agreements signed between the Portuguese and the local African rulers in the nineteenth century.[44]

Sucessionist aspirations of the Fernando Poo Bubis were also in part a result of the fact that until 1963 Fernando Poo and Rio Muni were two distinct colonial entities. Even the Moroccans and Libyans who very often lash out against the "colonialist" boundaries which stand in the way of a Greater Morocco or a Libyan-led pan-Saharan Arab state very often resort to colonial history to argue their case. The Moroccans, for example, insist that various colonial treaties (e.g., the Spanish-Moroccan Treaty of 1861, the Anglo-Moroccan Treaty of 1895, and the Franco-German Treaty of 1911) recognized Moroccan sovereignty in the Western Sahara. Their claim to the Tindouf area in Western Algeria is also based on the fact that it was administered until the 1950s by the French colonial administration in Morocco and not as part of French Algeria.[45] The Libyans, too, base their claims to territories in Chad, Niger, and Algeria on the 1935 French-Italian Treaty of Rome.[46]

Although several African nationalist conferences (e.g., the All-African Peoples' Conference [AAPC] in Accra in 1958 and the Afro-Asian Peoples Solidarity Organization Conference in Moshi in 1963) adopted resolutions condemning the colonial borders, it is clear from the proceedings of the conferences that the resolutions were more in support of specific revisionist movements—for example, the Kamerun and the Greater Somalia movements—than of revisionism in general. In addition, it should be kept in mind that the Camerounian nationalists, who were largely responsible for the Accra Resolution, aimed only at the substitution of one colonial border for another. Demands for the establishment of wider units in the name of national self-determination may also be based on the perception of one colonial self which is larger than the post-colonial state. The battle cry of African nationalists was for many years "Africa for the Africans," and for the pan-Africanists, that meant a pan-African state (or a "United States of Africa") for the pan-African nation. The rationalization for this pan-nationalism was neither linguistic, cultural, nor racial, but rather the common colonial experience. The pan-national self was defined by the essential similarities of all colonialisms.

Regionalists also want to abolish the present states and create larger units. They want to create a wider national-self by combining territories which were wholly or partially united under colonialism. An example from the last years of decolonization are the efforts of many Francophone African leaders to achieve independence within the French West African Federation (AOF) and the French Equatorial African Federation (AEF). In Central Africa, Barthelemy Boganda worked to establish the "United States of *Latin* Africa" comprising the AEF, the Belgian Congo, Cameroun, Equatorial Guinea, and Angola, all of which were ruled by "Latin" colonial governments.[47] Aspirations in the 1960s to establish an East African Federation were essentially based on the assumption that these territories had much in common because they shared the experience of British colonial rule. Almost all Africans affirm the importance and decisiveness of colonial history and at least some colonial self in African nation building. Certainly there are also efforts in Africa to resort to ethnocultural, precolonial-historical, and geographic selves for the sake of self-determination, but it should be kept in mind that the colonial self is dominant in postcolonial Africa.

The Ethnocultural Nation

A different kind of self for whom the demand for national self-determination is sometimes voiced is the ethnocultural group—the "tribe" in colonial terminology. The ethnocultural group is difficult to define. For many people, ethnicity evokes strong emotions and dominates their collective identity and solidarity. To Rothschild, "the ethnic group is somewhat analogous to Robert Frost's definition of home—the place where when you have to go there, they have to take you in."[48] The ancient Greeks were fully aware of the distinction between polis and ethnos. The ethnocultural self may be based on language (e.g., Germans and Italians), religion (e.g., Jews and Pakistanis), racial differences (e.g., Malays and Chinese in Malaysia or blacks and Indians in Guyana), or the more vague concepts of culture, tradition, and way of life. In the nineteenth and twentieth centuries, the nation-state, as a state where state and nation overlap, became a universal ideal. There are two basic ways to achieve the nation-state: one is by amalgamating through "integration nationalism" different ethnocultural selves within an existing state (as was done historically in Western Europe), and the other is to achieve independence through "separatist nationalism" for a preexisting ethnocultural self (as was done between 1820 and 1920 in the Balkans and Eastern Europe). Thus, not all ethnocultural groups develop a nationalism with demands to be defined as nations which have the right to self-determination. Some ethnic groups will gradually assimilate and integrate in a given state. But some will not, and as long as the ethnocultural selves exist, they have the potential to switch from integration nationalism to separation nationalism.

Very often, the nationalism of an ethnocultural group (nationalism with nation) can more easily mobilize a preexisting, underlying mass sentiment than a state-based nationalism devoid of ethnocultural content (nationalism without nation).[49] Today, as in the nineteenth century, and in the Third World, as well as in Europe or the Soviet Union, "ethnic nationalism proposes a radical alternative legitimation and rationale for the world political system to the prevailing statist framework."[50] The tension between statist national self-determination and ethnic national self-determination in Africa follows the nineteenth century European pattern of conflict between states (e.g., Austria-Hungary, Czarist Russia, the Ottoman Empire, and Great Britain) and nations (e.g., Italians, Czechs, Serbs, Poles, Greeks, Irish).

As in nineteenth and twentieth century Europe, the majority principle is ill equipped to deal with the problems of a state containing dissatisfied ethnocultural groups who demand the right of national self-determination. Arend Lijphart has observed that "majority rule works well when opinions are distributed unimodally and with relatively little spread . . . when there is considerable consensus and majority and minority are not far apart."[51] Where there are permanent ethnocultural majorities and minorities, the majority has no incentive to allay the minorities' grievances, and the minority will be disillusioned with a principle which condemns it to permanent exclusion from the levers of power and influence. Nordlinger says that the application of the majoritarian principle in a plural society may even contribute to conflict exacerbation rather than facilitate conflict regulation.[52] If a minimal national consensus is missing, as it was in Czarist Russia, Austria-Hungary, and pre-1921 Great Britain, as it is today in most African states, then the preconditions for majoritarian democracy do not exist. An example is the explanation given by an Arab Sudanese for Southern secessionism: "The Southerners *because in the minority* and apprehensive of domination by the Arabs of the North defined self-determination to mean separate independence for the North and the South."[53]

In Africa, most of the states contain a host of ethnocultural groups. Very few states are unilingual (Somalia, Rwanda, Burundi, Malagasy Republic, Lesotho, Botswana) and even some of these are badly split into hostile communal groups (e.g., the Tutsi-Hutu cleavage in Rwanda and Burundi). Most of the African states "share little but their own variety."[54] The states themselves are usually not distinct from each other in any cultural differentiae. Very few states are ethnoculturally homogeneous, and even in some of these cases, the cultural nation which preceded the state may not overlap with the political nation which is a product of the state. The ethnocultural groups may be of different sorts. Most frequently they may be defined by language (Kikuyu, Oromo, Baluba, Yoruba) or a mix of language and religion (Hausa-Fulani, Arab Sudanese, Somalis, Amhara). Sometimes racial differences play a major role—the Europeans in preindependence Algeria, Angola, Rhodesia, and Kenya and in present-day South Africa. But racial differences have also played a major role in defining ethnocultural groups in independent Africa. The distinctions between Arabs and Africans in Mauritania, Sudan, and prerevolution Zanzibar; between Touaregs and Africans in Mali and Niger; and between Hutu and Tutsi in Rwanda and Burundi are based on physical differentiae and not only on cultural characteristics.

While not all ethnocultural groups in Africa demand recognition as na-, tions, the racially tinged notion that ethnocultural groups in Europe are nations, while in Africa they are tribes must be rejected. Certainly 75,000 Luxembourgers or 500,000 Basques do not deserve to be regarded as nations any more than the Ibos, Yorubas, Oromos, Bakongo, or Zulu who number in the millions.[55] The numbers game also makes it illogical to talk of tribes as small nations, because while some of the populations called tribes are small, others are fairly large. As described before, opposition to ethnic self-determination has led many African leaders to deny the national character of ethnic groups and thus to deny their existence as legitimate national selves with a right to self-determination. The opposite occurred when Nyerere recognized Biafra. He specifically insisted that the major Nigerian ethnocultural groups—the Ibos, the Yorubas, and the Hausas—were not tribes, but nations, and as such were entitled to national self-determination.

Quests for ethnic self-determination in Africa since the 1950s have been relatively rare. In the 1950s the *Alliance des Bakongo* (ABAKO) wanted to reunify in a revived Kongo state the Bakongo people who were divided by the colonial partition of Africa between the French Congo (the Congo Republic), the Belgian Congo (Zaire), and Angola. ABAKO started as a linguistic movement, an "association for the maintenance, unity and expansion of the Kikongo language," and developed later into an ethnic political party.[56] Similar aspirations for a Bakongo state were voiced in the early 1960s by Congo-Brazzaville's first president, Fulbert Youlou, and by the Angolan *Frente Nacional de Libertacao de Angola* (FNLA) leader Holden Roberto.

The Oromo movement in Ethiopia which developed in the 1970s wants "the realization of national self-determination for the Oromo people and their liberation from oppression and exploitation."[57] The Oromos, whose sense of nationhood is based on common language, traditions, and a myth of common origin, founded the Oromo Liberation Front (OLF) which wants to establish in the Oromo-inhabited regions of Ethiopia a "People's Republic of Oromia." Another example of ethnocultural separatism is the effort of the Sara in southern Chad to deal with the loss of power in Ndjamena in the late 1970s by "detachment of the Sara speaking communities from the formal political space once occupied by the Chadian state."[58] The Gabonese Fang also voiced claims to be united with their fellow Fang in Rio Muni (before Rio Muni was united with Fernando Poo to form Equatorial Guinea). From time to time, demands for ethnocultural self-determination were voiced in all parts of Nigeria—North, East, and West. In the 1950s, Ibo leaders talked about the Ibo nation's right to constitute a sovereign Ibo state.[59] In the 1960s, Ibos demanded also that Nigeria take over Fernando Poo, where a large migrant Ibo population resided.[60] In the Southern Cameroon, the Cameroons Peoples National Convention (CPNC) demanded a partition along ethnic lines because in the 1961 plebiscite the Ibo-related western part of Southern

Cameroon opted for Nigeria and not for Cameroun.[61] In Western Nigeria, Yoruba nationalists demanded unification with their fellow Yorubas in Dahomey (Benin).[62] In Northern Nigeria and Niger, similar demands for Hausa unity were voiced in the 1950s and 1960s.

In Togo, there existed side by side with the Togoland unification movement an Ewe nationalist movement to unify all the Ewes residing in the former British and French Togo and in Ghana (Gold Coast) and Benin (Dahomey).[63] The Ewe self in this case is different from the colonial Togoland self: a pure Ewe nation-state would have included the southern portions of the two Togos and some areas in Ghana and Benin, while a united Togoland would have included both the Ewe and non-Ewe areas of the two Togos and excluded the Ewe areas of Ghana and Benin. TOLIMO, active in Ghana's Ewe areas in the 1970s, called on Ghana "to let the people go to join their 'kith and kin' in the Republic of Togo."[64] Nkrumah's Ghana also advocated incorporation of the divided Ewe and Agni in one state—but in the state of Ghana. The secessionists in Mayotte regard the Mahorais as a distinct ethnocultural self, different by ethnic origin, language, culture, and religion from the other Comorians. Indeed, while Grande Comoro, Moheli, and Anjouan have a "Zanzibari" character (Afro-Arab and Muslim), Mayotte is primarily Christian, and by language and culture, Malagasy. Mayotte also has a stronger Creole ingredient and regards itself as more French than the other islands (which explains why it opted to remain French rather than to choose independence).[65]

Another ethnocultural self is racial pan-Africanism as opposed to continental pan-Africanism. Racial pan-Africanism regards the whole of black Africa as a relevant self for self-determination. Originally, African nationalism was indeed race oriented and not territory oriented. People talked about African nationalism in the Gold Coast, Nigeria, or Kenya and not about Gold Coast, Nigerian, or Kenyan nationalism. In this case, racial similarity and solidarity replaced any linguistic, religious, or cultural identity. Racial pan-Africanism was potentially revisionist and opposed to an independent Africa divided by colonial borders. In the 1940s and 1950s, it was still a formidable emotional and political force. In the 1960s pan-Africanism both expanded and contracted. It expanded geographically to include the Arab states of North Africa, but it contracted in the sense that it lost its momentum to achieve the complete political unification of Africa. With the foundation of the OAU, which is a continental association of independent states, pan-Africanism became both continental and state oriented. Yet it is too early to dismiss the possibility of a resurgence of black pan-Africanism which will be directed both against the continentalism and statism of the OAU.

In the Western Sahara dispute, there are forces in Mauritania and within POLISARIO which call for self-determination and unification of all Hassaniya-speaking Arabs (called Saharwi, beidan, or ahel al sahel) living in the Western Sahara, the Tarfaya province of Morocco, the Tindouf area of Algeria, and North-West Mali. The former Mauritanian president Mokhtar Ould Daddah used to speak about the "common language, traditions, customs" and "desert civilization" of all Hassaniya-speakers which makes the abolition of the "artificial" boundaries and "reunification" a necessity.[66] Libya's Mu'ammar Qadhdhafi also rejects the colonial boundaries which divide "brothers" and calls for unification of all Sahara Arabs (which, in his eyes, includes not only the Arabs proper but also the Islamized and partially Arabized peoples like the Touareg, Berbers, Toubous, Kanembous, and Massalit, but not black African Christians and traditionalists like the Sara of Chad and the Dinka of Southern Sudan) as a first step towards Arab unity. Pan-Arabism itself is a call for self-determination by the Arab "*qa'umiyya*" (nation) in opposition to what is regarded as artificial states which oppress Arabs and prevent them from following their natural inclination towards Arab unity. In that sense, pan-Arabism is very different from continental pan-Africanism which lacks a common ethnocultural base.

The cases of Somali irredentism, Southern Sudanese secessionism, and Afar nationalism are slightly different. In these cases, the driving force is certainly ethnocultural nationalism, but in all of them the defined self is not purely ethnocultural. The Somali goal of a Greater Somalia calls for the unification of all Somali territories in the name of ethnocultural self-determination. Underlying this demand is the strong conviction and feeling that the Somalis in Somalia, the Ogaden Region of Ethiopia, the former Northern Frontier District of Kenya, and Djibouti are one national self. Former Somali president Haji Mohammed Hussein emphasized that "we are the same geographically and racially. We have the same language and the same religion. There is no future for us except as part of a Greater Somalia."[67] Somalis define their nation in terms reminiscent of nineteenth century European nationalism. It is defined by Hussein Adam as a people inhabiting a contiguous territory and possessing a common language, culture, history, and tradition with Islam providing "an important ingredient of their common culture."[68] Somalis perceive the Somali nation in Somalia, Ethiopia, Kenya, and Djibouti as one organism. A popular Somali liberation song asks "how can an amputated man sleep comfortably at night?"[69] Somali nationalism is determined never to "sleep" until the "amputated" parts are "returned" to Somalia. As in Italian, German, and Polish nineteenth century nationalism, for Somalis, national self-determination means that the whole Somali ethnocultural nation should be united in one state. In 1981, Somali Information Minister Mohamed Sheikh declared that all Somalis "are one and have the right to be unified."[70] Their aim is to create one state for an existing nation and not to build a nation within an existing state as is the case in most African states. In the name of the right of the Somali nation to self-determination and unity, regardless of the colonial boundaries, British

Somaliland and Italian Somalia were united in 1960. The constitution as well as the five star flag of the Somali Republic maintain the demands for a "union of all Somali territories."[71] Nevertheless, in at least two cases, the Somali irredenta is not purely ethnic and involves a hidden recognition of colonial selves as indivisible units for self-determination. The Somalis regard the whole of Djibouti as part of Greater Somalia, although the northern part of this former French colony is not peopled by Somalis. Similarly, they regard as Somali territory the whole former NFD of Kenya, although it is not all Somali. In fact, some of the ethnic groups in the western part of the NFD opposed any association with Somalia in the 1962 "consultations."

The Afar case is similar in many ways. The Afar Liberation Movement (ALM) wants to create a 'Greater Danakilia' uniting the Afars of Djibouti (ca 100,000) and the Afars living in Eritrea, Tigre, Wollo, and Hararge (ca 500,000).[72] Pan-Afarism, like pan-Somalism, is ethnocultural nationalism espousing self-determination, independence, and unity for the Afar nation. Unlike the Somalis, the Afar do not have a nation-state of their own although they share the binational state of Djibouti which is composed of Somalis and Afars. Like the Somalis, the Afars recognize some legitimacy of the colonial selves because they too claim the whole of Djibouti including the Somali-inhabited southern part.[73]

The quest for national self-determination in the Sudan is basically ethnocultural. Although the peoples of the Southern Sudan belong to different ethnocultural groups or tribes (Dinka, Madi, Shilluk, Zande, etc.) speaking different languages and inhabiting distinct ethnic homelands, the South feels that in comparison to the North it still has much in common. The Southern Sudanese leader, Bona Malwal, summed up the basic differences between North and South: "There is very little in common between Northern and Southern Sudanese. Basically, the North is Arab, the South is Negroid; religiously the North is Muslim, the South is pagan, linguistically the North speaks Arabic and the South some eighty different languages."[74] Northern Sudanese see themselves as part and parcel of the Middle Eastern Arab-Muslim civilization, while the Southern Sudanese perceive themselves as part and parcel of black-African civilization. Racial differences play an important role in defining the Southern Sudanese self. The Southerners' struggle for self-determination is seen as necessary "to preserve their negroid personality and identity."[75] Malwal also insists that the great divide is racial-cultural ("Africanity" versus "Arabness") and not religious (the few Southern Sudanese Muslims supported the South).[76] The gap between North and South is wide, and one of Africa's bloodiest wars of secession raged in the South between 1955 and 1972. The war was terminated in 1972 by the Addis Ababa Accords but erupted again in the 1980s.

In spite of the openly declared ethnocultural character of the Anyanya struggle, the perception of the Southern self is not completely ethnocultural. The South defines itself as comprising the three former colonial provinces of Upper Nile, Equatoria, and Bahr-al-Ghazal. The boundary between North and South is not strictly racial-cultural, for it leaves some black African groups in the North (e.g., the Nuba of Western Sudan). Nevertheless, the Southern Sudanese nationalists did not insist on incorporating the Nuba Mountains into an independent Southern Sudan. Again, some legitimacy was accorded to colonial-administrative boundaries, and the territorial claims were not defined strictly in racial, ethnic, or religious terms.

In Katanga, the forces for separatism were the Swahili-speaking Lunda and Bayeke who belong by culture and outlook to East Africa, while their main opponents in Katanga (the Baluba and Tshokwe) are by language and tradition part of Congolese civilization. In the Katangan case, secession was sought for the whole Katangan colonial-administrative self, but the separatist forces had a well-defined ethnocultural identity.

South Africa's policy of developing ethnic homelands into independent ethnocultural nation-states cannot be regarded as a case of ethnocultural self-determination. The case of the Transkei, Ciskei, Bophutatswana, Venda, or Kwazulu is different, because the basic demand for secession and independence does not come from "below"—from the Xhosa, Tswana, or Zulu—but from "above," from the South African government. Essentially, the government employed a divide and rule strategy by declaring that South Africa's blacks consist of many nations (and by not applying the same logic to South Africa's whites). Thus, these cases differ completely from the ethnic movements of the Oromo, Afar, Somali, or Mahorais. They reflect the needs of the ruling Afrikaners more than the aspirations of the Africans in the homelands. Their independence, whether real or fictitious, may be better dubbed other-determination than self-determination. The same can be said with regard to South Africa's attempt in the 1960s to follow a policy of "self-government for native nations" in Namibia.

In addition to the classical tension between the statist self and the ethnocultural self (e.g., Ethiopia versus Oromo, Sudan versus Southern Sudan, the Comoros versus Mayotte), the very identity of the ethnocultural self may be in dispute. An example is the tension between Oromos and Somalis in Ethiopia. The Western Somali Liberation Front (WSLF), which was founded in the 1960s, claimed that the Oromos and Somalis in Ethiopia are related groups and essentially one people because both speak similar Cushitic dialects, believe in Islam, and share the Amhara enemy. On the basis of the similarity between Oromos and Somalis, the WSLF and the Somali government demanded that Ethiopian provinces like Hararge, Arusi, Bale, and Sidamo, which have a mixed (Oromo and Somali) population, be included in Greater Somalia. In 1977, the Somalis went a step further by founding the Somali Abbo Liberation Front (SALF) which argued that the Oromos are part of the Somali national self. The Oromos were now called "Abbo Somalis" while the true Somalis were called "Wariya Somalis" ("Abbo" and "Wariya" means "you" in Somali and Oromiya, which were declared to be Somali dialects). The SALF was led by the old-time Oromo guerilla leader Wago Gutu, who now Somalized his name to become Ibrahim Waago Gutu Usu.[77] The Somalis went as far as "assimilating the Oromo within the Somali national genealogy as descendents of the ancestor of the Hawiye and Dir Somali clan families."[78] Between 1977 and 1978, Somalia also suppressed Oromo nationalist exiles in Somalia who disagreed with the official policy of Somalizing the Oromos. The Oromo nationalists represented by the OLF talked about self-determination for the Oromo nation and rejected Somali territorial demands for Ethiopia's Oromo inhabited provinces. It is significant that while the SALF leadership was Muslim, the OLF commanders were mainly Christian. Nevertheless, in this case, two nationalisms—one pan-Somali, the other pan-Oromo—argue that the same ethnocultural group belonged to different national selves for the purposes of national self-determination. In addition to Oromo nationalists and Oromos who identify as Abbo-Somalis, there were Amharized Oromos who identified as Ethiopians and rejected both Somali irredentism and Oromo separatism. In the same way, Somalis identified as part of the Somali nation or regarded the clan (e.g., the Issa) or the territorial subgroup (e.g., the Ogadenees) as the proper self for self-determination. Some Somalis (and Eritreans) even identified as Arabs. Similar internal divisions and conflicting identities among ethnocultural groups exist among the Bakongo, Southern Sudanese, Sara, Yoruba, and Ibo.

A variant of ethnocultural self-determination is "communal self-determination," which is defined as the aspiration of a communal group to determine the sovereignty of an area which contains other communal groups without absorbing them within the national self. While, for example, in Spain the ruling majority recognized Basques and Catalans as part of one Spanish nation, the same was not true in Czechoslovakia or Cyprus. In interwar Czechoslovakia, the Sudeten Germans were not regarded as part of the Czechoslovak nation, but nevertheless the Czechoslovaks did not accord them the right of national self-determination as a separate nationality. In Cyprus, prior to 1960, Greek-Cypriot nationalism denied that Greek and Turkish Cypriots were one people but nevertheless supported "*enosis*" which would have made the whole island part of Greece.

In Africa, in colonial times, the settler population in Algeria tried to make the whole country French by minority self-determination. The same is true for the Kenyan settlers who wanted, in the heart of Africa, self-determination for the European minority and the establishment of a "White Dominion." UDI-Rhodesia and apartheid South Africa are other examples where the European minority claimed national self-determination not for a territorially concentrated European population but for the whole country without respecting the wishes of the African majority. Former South African Prime Minister J.G. Strijdom talked about the European "right" to keep South Africa as *a whole* "a white man's country."[79] The Algerian, Kenyan, Rhodesian, and South African examples may also be defined as "racial self-determination" by a dominant minority. ("Master race self-determination" would be an appropriate term because the white minority claimed to determine the fate of the whole territory because of its alleged superiority.)

In the era of decolonization, the African majorities defined national self-determination as "majority self-determination." "Africa for the Africans" was in essence "Africa for the black African majority." Nkrumah emphasized that the Europeans and Indians in Africa might stay, but "they must respect us and our right as a majority to rule."[80] Other African nationalists shared Nkrumah's attitude towards the non-African minorities. They supported interracial tolerance and equal rights and did not advocate the expulsion of the non-African minorities. But none of them regarded the non-Africans as part of the national community in the emotional, as opposed to the legal, sense of the word. The very use of the terms "minorities," "settlers," "non-Africans," "those of foreign origin residing in Africa," "immigrant races," and "foreigners" reveals the perception of the whites and Indians as distinct communities whose real home is outside Africa and who are temporary guests in black Africa.[81] It would never occur to African leaders to employ the same terms to describe black Africans who moved some generations ago from one part of Africa to another. This distinction is significant because black African "settlers" and "immigrants" are often accepted, absorbed, and assimilated.[82] The same is not true across the color line. The blame for this lies mainly in the racial, and even racist, attitude of the settlers and immigrants themselves. This does not change the fact that the racial minorities are not included in the African national self. Nkrumah, Mboya, Nyerere, and Kenyatta all emphasized that the postcolonial states were black African states with a ruling black majority. Nonblacks had minority rights, as had many nationalities around the world, but there was no question of them being integrated in the African national community. In UDI-Rhodesia and apartheid South Africa, African nationalism sees the self as communal—it is the black African majority. The question in these cases is not in what territory self-determination should take place, but who are the people in the territory who constitute the appropriate self for self-determination. Those white-ruled states were not recognized by Africans as examples of genuine sovereign external self-determination or of democratic internal self-determination. The bone of contention in these cases has never been national-territorial sovereignty, but racial-communal self-determination.

That national self-determination could mean completely different things for the majority and for the minority could be seen after World War I when Africans and Afrikaner delegations appeared in the peace conference and both argued for South African national self-determination.[83] In the settler colonies, there was a complete reversal of the meaning of self-determination. In 1922, fifteen thousand white voters determined the external sovereignty of Rhodesia. In 1923, they were granted internal self-government for the territory as a whole without consulting the African majority. In 1953, fifty thousand white Rhodesians and a token five hundred blacks voted to found the Central African Federation. In 1965, the European minority even declared complete independence in the name of national self-determination. Fifteen years later, white-ruled Rhodesia became black-ruled Zimbabwe. Minority self-determination was replaced by majority self-determination. South Africa is the last bastion of European minority self-determination.

The distinction between minority and majority racial-ethnic self-determination may be also applicable to some intra-African conflicts. The 1960 revolution in Rwanda, the 1964 revolution in Zanzibar, and the 1980 revolution in Liberia were acts of majority self-determination against minority rule by the Arabs in Zanzibar, the Tutsi in Rwanda, and the Americo-Liberians in Liberia. In a similar way, the efforts to follow a policy of Arabization and Islamization in the Sudan and Mauritania could be perceived as majority self-determination which disregards the different wishes and identities of the non-Arab minorities.

Historic and Geographic Selves

Another self for which self-determination, independence, and reunification is sometimes demanded is a "historical national self," whether real or mythical. Most nineteenth century European nationalists understood the nation they fought for as a traditional-historical community. That is certainly true for traditional nationalists who conceived of the nation as a historical personality linking past, present, and future generations and as a group whose members share a "common cemetery."[84] For conservative nationalists, a nation was characterized by institutions and customs which represented the accumulated historical wisdom and experience of past generations.[85] Liberal nationalists also defined the nation as a historical community—as a community which has "done great things together" and has had "common memories, sacrifices, glories, afflictions and regrets."[86] The nationalists understood very well that "you cannot instill in a people a sense of kinship and brotherhood without attaching them to a place they feel is theirs, a homeland that is theirs by the right of history."[87] The historical definition of the national self was not only characteristic for nationalists of all shades and persuasions but was also shared by non-nationalists like Hegel, Acton, and Marx.[88] The demand for national self-determination in the name of an historic self was a powerful ingredient of German and Italian nationalism in the nineteenth century and of Polish, Czech, Hungarian, and Croat nationalism after World War I. In all these cases, the demands for the restoration of an historic state within its historical boundaries would have led to an expansion of the state beyond the ethnocultural boundaries.

African anticolonial nationalism adopted the ideas of the European enlightenment and presented its cause as enlightened and democratic. The slogans of anticolonialism were similar to those of the democratic revolution in Europe: equality, government by consent, sovereignty of the people, self-determination, and independence.[89] In addition, anticolonial nationalism, like any other national movement, was bound to resort to history in order to demonstrate that colonial conquest and occupation replaced precolonial freedom and independence. Anticolonial African nationalism aimed to restore, although in modified form, a golden age which had come to an end abruptly through foreign conquest.[90] In that sense, African anticolonialism was not different from any other modern nationalism. The question is in what sense precolonial history has played, plays, and will play a role in post-independence African nationalism. Anticolonialism was not based on a denial of history, but its success raised a serious dilemma. On the one hand, Africans have fully recognized that "every nation builds its future on its past."[91] On the other hand, however, very few of the postcolonial states have possessed a sufficient common precolonial history to build on. The colonial period left a deep and profound impact, but it was of relatively short duration. Thus the postcolonial independent state faced historic nations which were, in almost all cases, smaller than the existing state. Only in the cases of Egypt, Tunisia, Morocco, Ethiopia, Lesotho, Swaziland, Rwanda, and Burundi do the present states come close to being identical with their precolonial predecessors.[92] The problem is of prime importance for another reason as well: it is well known that during periods of modernization in which people are uprooted from their traditional environments, a "feeling of continuity" is essential to the stability of a society.[93]

History is hardly an objective, clearly discernible test for the existence of a national self. Even for the well-established nations of Europe, most of the objective common history covers less than two centuries, although subjective national myths greatly expand the period of common national experience. For nationalists, history has always meant, in fact, selective history. Nationalists, whose objective it is to foster a sense of identity and solidarity, to establish a chain of heroes, or to prove their case for a certain historical boundary, pick up those raisins from the cake of history which support and rationalize their cause.

Some of the secessionist movements in postcolonial Africa referred to precolonial historic nations. The numerous separatist and irredentist aspirations and claims in postcolonial Africa have revealed that the memory of historic states is alive, and that history provides a potential rationale for revisionism. The Baganda, Lozi, and Agni based their claims for separate statehood on their precolonial historic states and on the agreements those traditional states concluded with the Europeans.[94] Separatist sentiments, demands, and threats in Northern Nigeria in the 1950s and 1960s reflected Northern nationalism based on the unity of the historic Fulani Empire. ABAKO aimed to restore the ancient Kongo Kingdom, for "Leopoldville, Brazzaville and the Lac Leopold area, Angola and Pointe Noire were an integral part of the ancient Kongo Kingdom, a state that was divided in 1885 at the Berlin Conference among France, Belgium, and Portugal."[95] The South Kasai secessionists adopted symbols of the old Luba Kingdom in order to express historical continuity.[96] In the same way, Moise Tshombe's Katanga appealed to Lunda and Bayeke memories of their ancient kingdoms. That was made easier by the fact that Tshombe was married to the daughter of the traditional paramount chief of the Lunda, and that the other strong man of Katanga, Minister of the Interior, Godfroid Munungo, was the grandson of Msiri, the legendary emperor of the Bayeke Kingdom. The Benin Republic, founded in September of 1967 by pro-Biafran forces among the Ibos and Edos of the Midwest Region, is a classic example of how precolonial history may be mobilized in a moment of crisis and opportunity. In his declaration of independence, Major Okonko talked about the past grandeur of ancient Benin.[97]

Even when secessionism cannot be based on a historic state, it may nevertheless be defended by resorting to precolonial history. The Southern Sudanese separatists argued that "throughout its past history . . . the South has never been an integral part of the Arab world."[98] The Southern secessionists also cited precolonial historical hostilities, including slave raiding of the African population by Arabs from the North, as compelling reasons for Southern Sudanese independence.[99] The Southern Sudanese leader, Aggrey Jaden, insisted that "North and South had *never* been one."[100] Biafra's Ojukwu reiterated again and again that Nigeria was "never" one country.[101] Ojukwu, Azikiwe, Okpara, and other Biafran leaders added a precolonial dimension to the Biafran struggle by fostering a Christian Ibo identity and by identifying their adversaries with Muslim *Jihads* and conquests in the nineteenth century. The Somalis refer to the endless chain of wars between the Christian Ethiopians and the Muslim Somalis in order to justify their claims that the Ogaden Somalis cannot be Ethiopians and by ethnicity and history deserve to be united with their fellow Somalis in Somalia. Similar arguments about precolonial autonomy and unity have been raised by Oromos, Tigrineans, Afars, and Ewes.

The Eritrean argument for separate statehood rests strongly on the refutation of the Ethiopian claims that Eritrea is part of historical Ethiopia. The Eritreans argue that for hundreds of years the Ethiopian Empire did not effectively rule Eritrea, that in the precolonial era the local rulers along the coast and on the inland plateau were largely independent, that Ethiopian invasions were always fiercely resisted by the Eritreans, and that history created a homegrown Eritrean culture and civilization.[102] Bereket Haile Selassie, a leading spokesman for Eritrean nationalism, epitomizes precolonial Eritrean historiography:

> The people of Medri Bahri (Land of the Sea) *never* accepted the rule of the Abyssinian kings from Gondar or Tigreans from neighboring Tigrai. There was *continuous* resistance.[103] (Italics added.)

> Eritrean nationalism is *not a new phenomenon.* It is *historically rooted* in the common struggle of the Eritrean people against diverse forms of alien rule.[104] (Italics added.)

Precolonial history mobilizes people for national self-determination and secession. Its mobilizing potential is powerful—as demonstrated in Ireland, Poland, Croatia, and the land of the Basques, as well as in Africa. African nationalists face a dilemma in seeking to reconcile bitter opposition to colonialism with acceptance of colonial boundaries. The existing reality makes it possible to represent separatism as historically well-founded and as true anticolonialism. Separatism may fail in most cases in the end, but its recourse to precolonial history indicates that colonialism did not erase the links and memories of precolonial history.

In many African states, historical research has emerged that is centered on tribal units, a phenomenon whose political potential it is as yet too early to assess, although it shows a remarkable similarity to cultural-national revival movements in Eastern Europe. All of these movements began when historians rediscovered a national history, when philologists revived dormant languages, and when the nationalization of history, literature, and language spilled over into the sphere of politics.

Secessionism is one form of revisionism, irredentism is another. European irredenta, whether German, Italian, Greek, Spanish, Russian, or Polish, has always been a combination of ethnic longing for national unification and of attempts to restore a historic state and historic boundaries sometimes far beyond ethnic boundaries. The same is true for African irredentism. All Somali leaders speak not only about "Somaliness" and the "right of self-determination," but also about "historic links," and "reclaiming lost lands."[105] The Ethiopians deny the legitimacy of the Somali claim not only by using the OAU position against revisionism and balkanization but also by the quasi-historical argument that the Somalis are not a nation because they lack a common history.[106]

Ethiopia itself—whether Haile Selassie's "empire" or Mengistu Haile

Mariam's revolutionary republic—has strong beliefs in a historical Ethiopian self. Ethiopia rejects secessionist self-determination for Eritreans, Somalis, Oromos, Tigrineans, and Afars because it recognizes only one historical Ethiopian self.

Ethiopia's unification with Eritrea in 1952 was seen by Ethiopians as a "return to the mother country" and not as annexation (as the Eritrean nationalists see it).[107] "The history of Eritrea has been one with Ethiopia," declared the Ethiopian government in 1945.[108] The historical definitions of the Ethiopian self have strengthened the resolve of Haile Selassie's and Mengistu Haile Mariam's governments to hold on to Eritrea.

The Ethiopian nationalists argue that the beginnings of Ethiopia as a state were in Eritrean Axum and that for a millenium it was the center of the kingdom. According to Ethiopian historiography, during the reign of the Solomonic dynasty, and even in the decentralized "era of the princes," Eritrea's local rulers always maintained ties with the Ethiopian center, or at least with Ethiopian Tigre.[109] The Ethiopians also deny the Eritrean claim to statehood by claiming that Eritrea is not a nation with a common history and an identifiable historic state.

Historical rationale, the wish to restore historical Ethiopia, was used by Haile Selassie in the 1960s to explain his annexationist ambitions towards Djibouti, "one of Ethiopia's lost provinces along the Red Sea."[110] In 1941, after Ethiopia's liberation from Italian rule, Haile Selassie talked about the restoration of "the independence of my country including Eritrea and Benadir (Somalia)."[111] As recently as 1949, Ethiopia's historical nationalism was advanced to demand the incorporation of the whole of Somalia into the Ethiopian Empire. In the 1960s, this claim was dropped, but the Ethiopian emporer recalled that "things would have been quite different according to history," thus indirectly maintaining the historic claim and its destabilizing potential.[112] In 1964, the Third Division of the Ethiopian Army commanded by Gen. Aman Andom was already on its way to Somali Hargeisa before the government decided not to invade. Again in 1978, the possibility of an Ethiopian invasion of Somalia was openly discussed, and it cannot be ruled out that an Ethiopian conquest would have revived the historical claims to Somali territory.

Irredentist claims may be raised and dropped, but they will always refer to precolonial history. An example is Banda's laying claim to parts of Zambia and Mozambique in order to restore the historical boundaries of Malawi.[113] Another example is Lesotho's claiming chunks of the South African Orange Free State for the purpose of reestablishing historical Lesotho.

The Moroccan irredenta, with its objective of achieving a Greater Morocco within Morocco's historical boundaries, is another example that precolonial history, goals, and sentiments are alive and well. The Moroccan irredenta has led to wars with Algeria and to the protracted bloody conflict in the Western Sahara. Essentially, the Moroccans wanted to restore the boundaries of the ancient Almoravid Empire of the eleventh and twelfth centuries. That goal led them at various times to claim the whole of Mauritania and the Western Sahara, portions of Algeria and Mali in addition to the already absorbed colonial territories (Spanish Northern and Southern Morocco, Tangier, and Ifni), and the Spanish enclaves of Ceuta and Melilla. In the 1960s, Morocco called independent Mauritania Morocco's "amputated part."[114] Istiqlal leader Allal al Fassi compared the idea of national self-determination for Mauritania with the notion that Liverpool or Marseilles should be granted the right to independent statehood.[115] The present war in the Western Sahara stems from a deep-seated Moroccan conviction that Moroccan Sahara is part of historical Morocco which Moroccan troops liberated in 1976. The Moroccans argue that in precolonial times, the tribes of the Western Sahara declared their allegiance to the Sultan of Morocco, whom they regarded as ruler and *amir-al'mu'minīn* (defender of the Faithful). They further stress that the Sultan appointed *qaids* (governors) of Western Sahara tribes by *zāhirs* (official pronouncements). The historical memories of "glories and conquests of precolonial Morocco" make the Sahara, for the Moroccans, part of their national self which they recovered and restored to Moroccan sovereignty.[116] Another North African example of historical irredentism is the Egyptian claim to the Sudan in the 1940s and early 1950s, a claim based on the perceived historical unity of the Nile Valley.

Not only the balkanizing forces but also those political leaders who have unified or attempted to unify territories did so in the name of history. The Senegalese and Soudanese leaders who established the Mali Federation in 1959 felt that they united two parts of one historic whole. Dia explained that the "Soudan and Senegal shared the same historical origins."[117] Senghor stressed the common historic heritage of supratribalism "as early as the era of the great Empires—Ghana, Mali and Songhai."[118] William Foltz commented that "Sudanese leaders define their task as one of taking up directly where the pre-colonial heroes like Samory left off."[119] When Nkrumah, Keita, and Touré established the stillborn United African States, they stressed the historic links between the territories which now make up Ghana, Mali, and Guinea.[120] The one success in interstate unification, the merging of Tanganyika and Zanzibar into the new state of Tanzania, had deep historical roots, and Sheikh Abeid Karume and Julius Nyerere were well aware of the historic links. Nyerere regarded the union of both countries as correcting an accidental deviation: "history tells us that at one time Zanzibar and a large part of mainland Tanzania were ruled by one Government . . . . It was an accident of history that we did not continue to be one country."[121]

Other projects to amalgamate territories with close historical links were the project to unify Senegal and Gambia and the plan to unify Guinea and Sierra Leone. In both cases, historic ties were cited to legitimize the idea of unification.[122] The establishment of confederal links between Senegal and Gambia in 1983 and the stationing of Guinean troops in Sierra Leone in the 1970s and 1980s demonstrate that the potential for unification definitely exists in these two cases. Thus, although the precolonial African states do not overlap with the present states, unifying projects resort to historiography. In Africa, the universal rule of modern nationalism, that "the 'past' is used to explain the present, to give it meaning and legitimacy," is as true as anywhere else.[123]

Separatism and both irredentist and expansive varieties of revisionism base their claims or support their acts *post factum* by resorting to precolonial history, but precolonial history is important not only for revisionist nationalism but also for status quo nationalism. The Africanization of state names in the former Gold Coast, Soudan, Rhodesia, Nyassaland, and Dahomey by the adoption of names of historic African kingdoms like Ghana, Mali, Zambia, Zimbabwe, Malawi, and Benin are, as one observer put it, "shaky historical reconstructions . . . to satisfy the appetite of historical identity."[124] As we have seen in the case of Malawi, the association of postcolonial states with historic kingdoms may include seeds for potential revisionism, although—or perhaps because—the historic link between the ancient kingdoms and the present states is weak (Historical Ghana and Benin were even in different areas than today's Ghana and Benin).[125]

A universal characteristic of any form of nationalism is the need for national myths about the origin of the nation, its unity in the past, its wars and heroes, its racial purity and moral ways, its "chosenness," and its creativity. Nationalism may be interpreted as an attempt to achieve a renaissance by rediscovering a communal past and regaining a mythical golden age.[126] Historical myths are a *sine qua non* of any modern nation. Without a national history, a modern nation can hardly exist. Thus, if history itself does not provide enough greatness, heroism, unity, and achievement, history has to be refurbished in order to serve the survival and grandeur of the nation. For African nationalism, because of colonial degradation and racial discrimination, the need for compensating myths is even more pronounced.[127]

Smith described nationalism as the "myth of historical renovation."[128] In all nationalist literature everywhere, we find the same nationalist-historical terminology: "rebirth," "renovation," "renaissance," "rediscovery," "return to roots," and "rejuvenation." This terminology indicates the inseparable linkage between nationalism and history. Pan-Africanism might appear at first glance as an exception, for as Thomas Hodgkin put it: "there is no African Mazzini . . . Africa exists as an idea only projected into the future, not as an historic fact. There has been no single comprehensive civilization, no common background of written culture to which nationalists could refer."[129] Historically, Hodgkin is correct, but his neglect of the role of myths led to his erroneous assumption that Africa does not exist in the minds of nationalists as a historical self. There is "no common background" to refer to, but the common background can be created and has been created in nationalist mythology. There are African leaders who believe in the myth of the precolonial unity of Africa, a unity which was destroyed by colonial partition and balkanization. Nyerere talks about the "feeling of unity on the continent . . . grown out of . . . pre-European history."[130] He does not call for the unification of Africa, but for its "reunification."[131] Nkrumah and Touré spoke about a common past of Africa and the need to "reunite" the "balkanized" continent.[132] Senghor propagated the cultural myth of "*africanité*" which combines "*négritude*" and *arabité*."[133] This pan-African cultural unity is, according to Senghor, "au-delà de l'histoire. Il est enraciné dans la préhistoire."[134] Senghor thus emphasized his belief in the precolonial cultural unity of Africa. Azikiwe even went as far as to claim that "conscious efforts have been made at all known times of African history to form a political union either on a regional or a continental basis."[135] No history books tell us about "conscious efforts" to unify the African continent "made at all known times of African history." Azikiwe is not the only African leader to mobilize history in order to prove that African unity is a logical consequence of precolonial history and thus inevitable and natural. After the agreement founding the Ghana-Mali Union, Nkrumah solemnly declared that "Ghana and Mali have historically always been one . . . The colonial powers tried to let our identity be lost to history but the generation of today is bound to resuscitate that identity and history."[136] The East African leaders who, in the early 1960s, supported the establishment of an East African Federation spoke about "reunification" of Kenya, Uganda, and Tanzania which, in their view, were artificially separated by colonialism.[137] That real history, as opposed to mythical history, shows us that colonialism drew the three countries closer together rather than farther apart seems to have been overlooked by Kenyatta, Nyerere, and Obote. These examples demonstrate also that in Africa myths about a common history may offer an effective substitute for real common history.

Revisionists are no less in need of historical reconstructions than leaders of existing states who strive to foster territorial national unity. ABAKO propagated the myth, refuted by historical research, that the old Kongo Kingdom included all the Bakongo living today in Zaire, Congo, and Angola. In Katanga's declaration of independence in July 1960, Tshombe spoke about the precolonial unity of Katanga based on the historical cooperation of the Baluba, Bayeke, and Lunda kingdoms whose "historic destiny had been linked for centuries."[138]

Somali nationalists speak about the "dismembered motherland," although it was more "dismembered" in precolonial times.[139] They aspire to reunification of the Somali territories, although they were far from unified before. Camerounian nationalists who led the struggle for reunification of the former German Kamerun argued that the whole of Cameroun has a common history "since the days of old Carthago." Um Nyobé even insisted that "tout le monde reconnaîtra que Dieu a créé un seul Cameroun."[140] The phenomenon of myth making is a universal ingredient of any nationalism, and Nkrumah, Senghor, Ojukwu, and Shermarke are no different than Danilevsky, Mazzini, Laménais, Gandhi, and Ferhat Abbas.[141]

The fact is that, in the vast majority of cases, there is very little overlap between the new states and the precolonial political units. The fear of anarchic fragmentation leads to an ambivalent attitude towards precolonial history. While Nkrumah bitterly attacked the colonial powers for having "artificially" partitioned the African continent and for disregarding the fact that the colonial boundaries did not "originate from ancient African civilization," he was at the same time the architect and ardent supporter of continental pan-Africanism—a concept with no precolonial legitimacy, and one which is essentially geographical and ahistorical.[142] Nkrumah recognized that when he said that in the pan-African context, geography rather than "accidents of history" are decisive.[143] On the other hand, in his conflicts with Togo and the Ivory Coast, and in his regional unification schemes, Nkrumah knew very well how to stress those accidents of history which could advance his cause. Senghor, who did not hesitate to invoke history to legitimize the Mali Federation, on another occasion attacked "those who invoke history to support their territorial claims," for "one can always answer by invoking more history."[144] In Senghor's opinion, history is a legitimate argument for agreed unification but is unacceptable as a moral basis for separatism and irredentist ambitions. Dia shared Senghor's ambivalent attitude towards precolonial history as a basis for a modern national self. Dia pointed out that "to be a nation" does not necessarily mean "to possess a past, a history."[145] On the other hand, Dia's support for the Mali Federation was put forward in precolonial-historical terms invoking the ancient unity of the Sudanic belt and the memory of the old African empires. Nyerere admits that "Tanganyika is not a traditional unit at all," while at the same time talking of pan-African unity as grounded in precolonial history.[146] This inconsistency and contradiction in the African leaders' associations of precolonial history and nationhood reflects a basic African dilemma. On the one hand, the need for nationhood is at the same time a need for history, for continuity and depth, for heroes and myths, and for a final refutation of the colonial legend that Africa has no history. On the other hand, the rediscovery of history can rarely serve to strengthen the present state-nation, for history is to a large extent fragmented and ethnic and contains many conflicts and wars between groups which now find themselves in the same state. It is true that every nationalism is selective in its use of history. Rénan observed that fellow-nationals "have done great things together," but they also "have forgotten a good many things."[147] European nationalists invoked history when it suited their claim

for historic states and historic boundaries and rejected history when it collided with principles of national unity and self-determination. The difference between Europe and Africa does not lie in the use, misuse, or disuse of
history in nationalist ideologies. The difference lies in the greater historic
depth of most European states, many of which have existed for centuries.
This is not the case for the African states. Thus, in recent European history,
states like Austria-Hungary or Spain which supported the status quo could
invoke as much selective history as their revisionist opponents, be they
Poles, Ukrainians, or Basques. In Africa, there is little precolonial history
which could be selected to defend the present status quo. The status quo
powers have to look for other lines of defense in order to withstand the opposition of revisionism. As we have demonstrated before, the other line of
defense has been provided by colonial history.

Sometimes the national self is at least partially determined by geography. In many nationalisms, territory plays a pivotal role. Belief in natural
frontiers like seas, rivers, and mountains facilitates the crystallization of a
national identity. A good example is Ireland: the fact that Ireland is an island
facilitated the consolidation of a strong national identity. Sometimes geographic distance contributed to the creation of new nations by accelerating
differentiation in culture, life-style, ideology, and economic interests. The
growth of an American and an Australian nation are two striking examples.
In Latin America, geographic distance and natural barriers between population centers encouraged the development of different nations in an area relatively homogeneous by language and culture.[148]

In Africa, too, geography plays a role in defining some national selves.
The fact that "salt water" separated Algeria from France or Angola from Portugal was certainly an important reason why all efforts to assimilate these
territories and to eradicate their separate identities were doomed to fail.
Geography determined that the African establishment did not apply the
principle of self-determination within colonial boundaries to enclaves like
Ifni (Morocco) and Sao Joao Batista de Ajuda (Benin). For the same reason,
the South West African People's Organization (SWAPO) and the OAU reject
the South African efforts to hold on to Walfish Bay after Namibian independence. With regard to islands, the attitude was different. There was strong
support for self-determination for the Comoros, Seychelles, Cape Verde Islands, Sao Tome and Principe, and the not yet independent Canary Islands
and Réunion. There are some other examples where geography played a
role in defining a national self. The 1961 partition of the British Cameroons
into two national selves in the decisive plebiscite was made possible by the
geographic separation of Southern and Northern Cameroons. In British Togoland, which is one contiguous territory, such a division into an Ewe-
dominated South and a non-Ewe North was not permitted. Cabindan
separatism is facilitated by the fact that it is geographically noncontiguous

with the rest of Angola. Bubi secessionist aspirations on Fernando Poo cannot be understood without taking into account the geographic distance of the island from mainland Equatorial Guinea (Rio Muni). Aspirations to absorb Fernando Poo within Nigeria also had something to do with the proximity of the island to the Nigerian coast. The same applies to Mahorais separatism on Mayotte. "Northern" or "Southern" identities in states like Ghana and Nigeria are also influenced by the totally different geographic environment. Slogans like "The North for Northerners" (in Ghana in the 1950s) or "One North, One People" (in Nigeria in the 1960s) reflected this kind of regional quest for self-determination. Katanga's geographical identity should also not be underestimated. Katanga was not only culturally and linguistically closer to East and Southern Africa than to the center of the former Belgian Congo but also by geographical proximity and communications. Sometimes irredentist aspirations are also strongly influenced by geography. Egyptian aspirations in the 1940s and 1950s to unify with Sudan were influenced by a perception of one geographic Nile Valley. Pan-Somalism is strengthened by the firm belief that geographically Greater Somalia is one. Somali leader Abdillali Ise described Greater Somalia as the "Somali peninsula" which is a "well defined geographic unit."[149] Ethiopian ultranationalists also claimed that by geography, the whole Horn of Africa including Somalia belonged to Ethiopia.[150] Senegalese claims to Gambia were influenced by the enclave nature of Gambia, which is surrounded by Senegal on all sides. Continental pan-Africanists certainly have a geographical concept of Africa in mind. In general, we may conclude that, as anywhere else, geography plays a role in Africa in differentiating national selves which might claim the right for self-determination and independence—whether by separation, irredentism, or unification.

Mixed and Conflicting Identities

The demand for "pure" enthnocultural self-determination is relatively rare. More common in Africa is the quest for "mixed" ethnic-territorial self-determination. That was true for anticolonial self-determination in those cases where the colonial self was based on a dominant ethnocultural core (e.g., the Mossi in Upper Volta, the Arabs in Morocco and Algeria, the Moors in Mauritania, the Bahutu in Rwanda, the Wolof in Senegal). In postcolonial Africa, most separatisms are of the mixed type. Self-determination is asked in these cases for a colonial self which contains a specific ethnocultural core. The Biafrans fought for an independent Eastern Nigeria, not for self-determination of an ethnic Ibo homeland. Ojukwu always emphasized the multiethnic character of Biafra. In his speeches, he never referred to "Ibos" but always to "Easterners." Biafra was based on an Ibo core which constituted about two-thirds of the population, but it also contained sizable minorities in the coastal areas (Ibibio, Efik, Ijaw). The boundaries of Biafra were administrative-colonial and not ethnic-cultural. In essence, Biafra was as much an entity demarcated and defined by colonialism as the whole of Nigeria. The main difference is that in Biafra the Ibos were dominant in what they felt was their nation-state, while in Nigeria, after the Northern-led coup of July 1966, the Ibos were completely out of power. Another important difference is that in Biafra the Ibos had a clear majority, and thus the national make-up of the seceding state resembled the *majority-minorities* model of the European nation-states. In Nigeria, on the contrary, there is the typical African *minority-minorities* situation in which every minority faces other minorities but no majority.

Another mixed ethnic-territorial separatist case is Eritrea, where for two decades several guerilla movements waged a bitter war for secessionist self-determination. The two main groupings in Eritrea which form the backbone of the EPLF and ELF are the Tigrinya-speaking Tigrinean Christians and the Tigre-speaking Muslims. Eritrean nationalism is based on these two main ethno-cultural groups and their opposition to Amhara rule. Nevertheless, the aim of the Eritrean nationalist movements is an independent Eritrea defined by the colonial boundaries of the former Italian colony. There are ethnic forces in Eritrea which call for ethnocultural self-determination of all Tigrineans in an independent and united Tigre or Muslim secessionists who would like to see a Muslim or Arab Eritrea, but these forces are much weaker than the mixed ethnic-territorial Eritrean nationalism. In Katanga, too, the movement for independence of multiethnic Katanga reflected a commitment to a mixed self. As a province in the Belgian Congo, Katanga was an administrative colonial self, and as in Biafra, one ethnocultural core group, the Lunda, was the principal supporter of secessionist self-determination.

There is no doubt that the mixed nature of Biafra, Eritrea, and Katanga greatly weakened their struggle for national self-determination. The minorities in Biafra assisted the Nigerian invasion and made it easier for the Nigerians to defend their cause before international public opinion. Typical for the Nigerian argumentation that Biafra's quest for self-determination lacks legitimacy because Biafra itself denies its minorities the right of secession is Enahoro's statement that "if the union of Nigeria is dissolved there are no legal bonds to tie together the Ibos and the coastal kingdoms and other tribes of Eastern Nigeria who would be entitled to self-determination as the Ibos are."[151] In Katanga, the Baluba opposed Lunda separatism and even instigated a countersecession from Katanga in the northern part of the province. They made it almost impossible for the Katanga "*gendarmerie*" to resist the Congolese-UN onslaught on Katanga. In Eritrea, the mixed nature of the self explains the fratricidal fragmentation in the secessionist camp. In Eritrea, too, the Ethiopians can count on the support of at least some ethnic groups (e.g., Kunama and Baria, who in the past were enslaved by some of the other Eritrean ethnic groups).

The official goal of POLISARIO in the Western Sahara, the establishment of a "Sahara Arab Democratic Republic" within the former colonial boundaries of the Spanish colony, is also basically a call for mixed ethnic-territorial self-determination. SADR would have a clear ethnocultural base, because most Saharwi belong to the Hassaniya-Arab linguistic and cultural grouping. One specific subgroup—the Reguibat—clearly seems to dominate POLISARIO and the SADR government in exile. Nevertheless, the boundaries for which POLISARIO fights would leave many Hassaniya groups in the neighboring states (Algeria, Morocco, and Mauritania). "Greater Mauritania," uniting the Western Sahara and Mauritania, would again be a mixed national self because although it would have a clear Hassaniya core majority, it would still include Mauritania's black-African minority and leave out the Hassaniya-speaking population of Southern Morocco and Western Algeria.

The movement to unify both Togos is another example of a mixed self, for it combines ethnocultural aspirations for Ewe unification with a commitment to the pre-World War I German colonial boundaries. If united, Togo would not be a Ewe nation-state, but the Ewe would definitely be the dominant force in such a state. In 1977, Togolese President Eyadema demanded from Ghana the return of former British Togoland and the transfer to a reunited Togo of the Ewe-speaking areas of Ghana proper up to the Volta River, which he defined as a natural frontier. These demands mix a colonial self (a united Togo), an ethnocultural self (Ewe unity), and the notion of a natural geographical self.

Very often, unification-nationalism also combines colonial units which are assumed to have some other real or mythical community. An example is Senegalese aspirations to unify with Gambia on the assumption that ethnically both states are very close. Indeed the same ethnic groups (Wolof, Fulbe, Serere, Mandingo, Diola, Sarakolé) populate both countries, although the dominant group is different in each state (Wolof in Senegal, and Mandingo in Gambia). In addition, the Senegalese also feel both countries to be geographically one. Another example is the emphasis on common Swahili culture in the Tanganiyika-Zanzibar union and the justification of the Mali Federation by the belonging of Senegal and Sudan to "one Northern Sudanese sub-race." Mixed selves have sometimes combined historical and ethnocultural selves. For example, the Tigre Peoples Liberation Front (TPLF) has fought for self-determination of historical Tigre, defined as Tigre province and the Tigrinean-speaking areas of Eritrea. The movement is clearly ethnocultural and centered around the Christian Tigrineans and their age-long enmity towards the Amharas. Nevertheless, the TPLF insists on the indivisibility of historical Tigre, which means that non-Tigrineans (e.g., Afar and

Saho) will also be included in an independent Tigre. The strong "Northern" identity in Nigeria which led to strong separatist feelings in the 1950s and 1960s is also a mixed self based on colonial boundaries (Northern Region), an historic state (Fulani Empire), and an ethnocultural core (Muslim Hausa-Fulani). In the 1960s, leaders in both Congos declared their support for a restoration of the ancient Kongo state—a historic state of one ethnocultural nation. In general, many of the historic states (e.g., Buganda, Barotse, and Sanwi) in precolonial Africa were ethnoculturally homogeneous, and aspirations to restore them were based on an historic nation-state. Precolonial Africa has also known "plural states" which were multiethnic but contained a dominant people. Historical Ethiopia, with its dominant Amhara (and sometimes Tigrinean) core, and the Fulani Empire, based on the Hausa-Fulani, are two examples. Opposition to secession from Ethiopia and separatist aspirations in Northern Nigeria in the 1950s and 1960s are both examples of struggles to maintain or achieve independence for an historic self dominated by an ethnocultural core.

Kedourie wrote that "humanity is not naturally divided into nations" and that "the characteristics of any particular 'nation' are neither easily ascertainable nor exclusively inherent in it."[152] In order to understand the problems of national self-determination in postcolonial Africa, it is crucial to perceive the numerous conflicts between the different national selves. These conflicts arise because there is no scientific definition of the nation and no generally agreed criteria for the characteristics of a nation. Some conflicts are within the same category: the Nigerian colonial self versus the Eastern Nigerian 'colonial self', the Ethiopian historical self versus the Tigrinean historical self, or the Somali ethnocultural self versus the Oromo ethnocultural self. Other conflicts are between different categories: the Moroccan historical self collides with the West Saharan colonial self, the Afar ethnocultural self conflicts with the Ethiopian historical self and with the Eritrean colonial self, while the geographical selves of Mayotte, Cabinda, and Fernando Poo are opposed to the colonial selves of the Comoros, Angola, and Equatorial Guinea. Almost all aspirations to statehood, from continental pan-Africanism to the separatism of tiny territories like Sanwi and Cabinda, can be explained as aspirations to national self-determination. Only the definition of the national self is different from case to case. Thus it is completely misleading to attribute commitment to the principle of national self-determination only to one party in the numerous wars and conflicts in postcolonial Africa. There is hardly a state in Africa where the colonial, ethnocultural, and historical selves coincide. Even the few historical states sometimes contain more than one ethnocultural self (Rwanda, Burundi, Ethiopia, Morocco), or do not contain the whole ethnocultural self (Lesotho, Somalia). It is precisely because both Moroccans and Saharwi, Ethiopians and Eritreans, Sudanese and Southern Sudanese, Nigerians and Biafrans, and even Afrikaners and Africans have believed in conflicting interpretations of national self-determination that the conflicts have been so bitter and bloody.

Those who firmly believe in the right to national self-determination usually declare their own nation to be "one and indivisible." The Africans are following the French Jacobin tradition which saw the nation as an "organic" whole, which is not amenable to partition. For Nigeria's first president, Nnamdi Azikiwe, Nigeria in 1960 was "indestructible, perpetual and indivisible."[153] For the Western Region leader Obafemi Awolowo, Nigeria in the civil war was "indivisible." One of Ghana's leaders declared that "no *portion* of Ghana can leave Ghana"—the part has no life independent of the whole. For King Hassan II of Morocco, "One Morocco" is indivisible, and it includes the annexed ("liberated," "unified") Western Sahara. For Kenya's government, the Somali region is part of Kenya and no separation is possible.[154]

The German nationalist Heinrich von Treitschke rejected any notion of self-determination for Alsace-Lorraine; what mattered was the "higher right" of self-determination of the German people as a "whole."[155] In the same way, African central governments opposed separatist self-determination for Eritrea, the Ogaden, Southern Sudan, Katanga, Biafra, Western Sahara, Sanwi, Mayotte, and Cabinda because all these areas were regarded as parts of an indivisible whole.

The notion that the nation is indivisible, which is common to many nationalists—whether American, French-Jacobin, pan-Arab, Moroccan, Ethiopian, or Somali—stands in startling contrast with historical-empirical reality. The perception of nations as indivisible is based on the fallacy that nationhood is something permanent. In reality, nations come and go, and national identity may expand, contract, or disappear. Perhaps the reason for the sanctity of the indivisible nation is rooted in the hidden knowledge that all nations are divisible.

"Natives," "Settlers," and the "Critical Date"

Another problem area with regard to who is the self concerns the differentiation between "natives" and foreign "settlers." In 1918, the French rejected a plebiscite in Alsace-Lorraine because between 1871 and 1918 there was an exodus of French natives and an influx of German settlers. Similarly, Arab nationalism regarded only native Palestinians and not Israeli settlers as legitimate ingredients of a Palestinian self. The Turks perceived the Greek Cypriots as settlers on an island which they regarded as an extension of Turkish Anatolia. Most recently, the Third World majority in the UN refused to grant the inhabitants of Gibraltar and the Falklands the right to self-determination because it saw them as foreign settlers on native Spanish and Argentinian territory. It is interesting that these standards were not applied to the Fiji Indians or the Chinese in Singapore. They were also settlers in foreign lands, but because they did not come from European-colonial countries, their right to self-determination (in the case of Singapore) or their right to share in self-determination (in the case of Fiji) was recognized as legitimate.

Who is a settler with no legitimate rights to be included in the self, and who is not? An important question to determine is whether there is a "critical date." When does a settler cease to be a foreigner with no rights to national self-determination and become a native part of a self with full rights to national self-determination? Time is important, but on the question of the critical date there is no agreement. The Gibraltarians who have inhabited the colony for 250 years are considered settlers by the UN, while the much more recently settled Fiji Indians are accepted as part of the Fiji self.

In Africa, the question of natives and settlers with regard to national self-determination has come up several times. In the French Territory of the Afars and the Issas (TFAI), a bone of contention in the 1960s was who is a native Somali and who is a foreign Somali. Because of the delicate balance in the TFAI between Afars and Somalis (Issas), and because Somalia aspired to incorporate the TFAI as part of Greater Somalia, the issue became for both Afars and Somalis a life and death matter. Only native Somalis were allowed to vote on the future of the territory. The French, who opposed Somali aspirations in the 1950s, attempted to define as many Somalis as possible as alien settlers who have no right to vote. In this way, they tried to tip the balance in favor of the Afars. While according to UN sources there was a Somali majority in the 1960s, the French census provided for an Afari numerical edge in the 1967 plebiscite on the future of the territory. Many Somalis were declared illegal aliens, were refused the right to vote, and some were even deported across the border.[156] In 1972, an investigating committee established that more than sixty percent of the population was Somali. In 1975, another wave of deportations of alien Somalis and the distribution of Djibouti identity cards to Afars who fled from Ethiopia again reduced the Somali share in the 1976 plebiscite. For Afar nationalists, all Somalis in Djibouti are foreign settlers on Afari land. In fact, until the twentieth century, all land in present-day Djibouti was in the Afari domain. Issa and Ghadaboursi Somalis came in large numbers as workers to Djibouti only after World War II. In that sense, the early colonial name given to the territory (*Côte Française des Somalis*) was indeed misleading. In Mayotte, too, in the 1970s there was increased tension between the separatist natives and the foreign settlers from the other Comorian islands. After the 1974 plebiscite, which the separatists narrowly won, supporters of Comorian unity were expelled. In this way the separatist majority was greatly increased in the 1975 plebiscite.

The Kenyan attitude towards the Somalis in Kenya's North Eastern Region is also based on the perception that they are recent settlers and thus have no right to determine the fate of the territory which they inhabit. The Kenyan government declared that the "claim that tribes of Somali origin have occupied this whole area since time immemorial is without foundation. In fact, Somali incursion and settlement in what is now the Republic of Kenya has taken place within a single human life span."[157] The Kenyans recognized the Somalis' right to stay in Kenya and their right to leave for Somalia (the so called right to nomadic self-determination), but they did not accept their demand to detach a part of the Kenyan territorial self and to transfer it to Somalia. A major reason for the Katanga secession was the determination of the "*Katangais authentiques*" to deny political power and economic privileges to the foreigners who flocked into Katanga from other parts of the Belgian Congo in order to share in its prosperity. Lunda resentment was, in particular, directed against the Baluba from Kasai province. The program of the secessionist *Confédération des Associations Tribales du Katanga* (CONAKAT) called for the disenfranchisement, economic discrimination, and even for a possible expulsion of all Kasai-Baluba from Katanga. Similar conflicts between Bakongo "locals" and Bangala settlers and between Lulua locals and Baluba settlers explain separatist tendencies among the Bakongo and Kasai-Baluba in the 1950s and early 1960s.

In the Western Sahara, the dispute over the issue of the critical date is different. A good part of the Saharwi population has fled and now lives in the Moroccan Tarfaya province and in the Tindouf area of Algeria. The Saharwis living in Morocco came there in the 1950s mainly for economic reasons and partially because of Spanish oppression. Those in refugee camps in Algeria left because of their opposition to Moroccan occupation. In any negotiations about self-determination by plebiscite in the Western Sahara, two crucial questions are whether the refugees will have the right to vote and what the critical date is for leaving the Western Sahara (e.g., if it is 1976, the refugees in Morocco will have no right to vote, while those in Algeria will). It is clear that Morocco will refuse any formula which will only enfranchise the anti-Moroccan refugees in Algeria.

"The definition of the self is not only space bound and group bound, it is also time bound."[118] In precolonial times, there was hardly any national identity and unity among the Ibos, Yorubas, Southern Sudanese, Western Saharans, Sara, or Eritreans, yet some of these peoples later developed an intensive nationalism which enabled them to fight for years for national self-determination. The national self may change even in a relatively short period. For example, in the early 1950s, most Christian Eritreans strongly felt Ethiopian, and their support for the Unionist Party, which advocated union with Ethiopia, brought about the UN decision to "return" Eritrea to Ethiopia. By the 1970s, Christian Eritreans turned against Ethiopia and adopted an Eritrean national identity. Erlich stresses the time factor when he calls Eritreanism "a *young* emotion and essentially a negation of Ethiopianism."[159]

In 1960, most Ibos' prime identity was either pan-Nigerian (among the elite) or local-tribal (among the rural population). By 1967 or 1968, most Ibos were strong believers in Eastern Nigerian or Ibo nationalism which sustained Biafra for three years. If the Biafran incursion into the Western Region in the early stages of the war had succeeded, Eastern Nigerian and Ibo nationlism could have transformed itself quickly and easily into Southern Nigerian nationalism. Thus, even in a short period of time, dramatic events can effect drastic changes in the national identity of a population. This phenomenon is not unique to Africa. For example, the Austrians also changed their basic identity between 1938 and 1945 from total identification with Germany to a reassertion of Austrian identity. In the Western Sahara, even scholars sympathetic to POLISARIO agree that if the territory had been integrated with Morocco in the 1950s, "Saharwi nationalism would not have emerged as a political force."[160] In the 1970s, none could any longer deny the existence of a strong Saharwi nationalism which has proved its mettle in a decade of war against the Moroccan army. Different national identities may rise and fall, become stronger and weaker, in different situations and at different times. Among the Saharwi, competing, conflicting, and fluctuating loyalties in the last decades include Moroccan, Mauritanian, Western Saharan, Hassaniya, Maghrebist, pan-Arabist, pan-Saharan, and pan-Islamic identities.

Sometimes decisions by the colonial authorities shortly before decolonization may alter the future national self. The Spanish colonies of Rio Muni and Fernando Poo were united as Equatorial Guinea in 1963, just five years before independence. Equatorial Guinea thus became a national self within colonial boundaries in 1968, although the Bubis of Fernando Poo opposed the amalgamation with the Fang of Rio Muni. Today, any secession by Fernando Poo would be condemned by the OAU as a violation of the hallowed OAU principle that the legitimate national self to be granted statehood is the colonial territory within the colonial boundaries *at the time of independence.*

In Africa, as elsewhere, there is no permanent national self. Someone's primary identity may be Ethiopian, Eritrean, or Tigrinean in Eritrea or Nigerian, Southern, Eastern, or Ibo in Iboland. It will be a function of time and context. Ronen is right to say that the switch from one identity to another is possible because all identities are optional weapons in the quest for self-determination.[161] The identity of the self, which is so crucial to the establishment of self-determination, may vary with time. Different times and different conditions may lead to different identities and to a different perception of "us" and "them." For example, religious persecution may lead to the development of a strong identity based on religion. At another time, language may become a dominant issue which may lead to the crystallization of ethnolinguistic identities and the depolitization of religion. "To the questions 'Who am I?' and 'Who are you?' the appropriate answer is, 'It depends.'"[162]

THE GOALS AND MEANS OF
SELF-DETERMINATION

The fundamental requirement inherent in the concept of self-determination is a procedure, not a preset outcome.

Lung-chu Chen, 1976[1]

Not all nationalists want complete sovereignty . . . but all want recognition of their right to the homeland.

Antony Smith, 1979[2]

Sovereignty is a means to an end, not the end itself.

Peter Calvert, 1976[3]

The problem of how to ascertain the wishes of the self remains inseparable from the questions posed earlier of who the self is and what it may determine.

Michaela Pomerance, 1982[4]

Sometimes people confuse self-determination and independence. The 1960 UN Resolution on Colonialism (GAR 1541) mentioned independence, free association, and integration as possible and legitimate goals of national self-determination, but Portugal's misuse of these options during the 1960s and 1970s (when it argued that its African colonies chose integration with Portugal as overseas provinces) caused the UN to view national self-determination and independence as synonymous. Although national self-determination has, since World War II, mostly led to independence, it has sometimes led to different patterns and formulas.

Colonial self-determination may take the form of independence, unification with another colony, attachment to an independent state, some form of association or complete integration with the mother country, and preservation of the colonial status. The extra-African examples are numerous: In a free referendum, Puerto Rico voted for association with the United States, thus granting its inhabitants U.S. citizenship, democratic rights, an elected governor and legislature, and the option to vote for independence at any time (in 1967, only 0.7 percent voted for independence, while 38.9 percent voted for statehood within the United States, and 60.5 percent for associa- tion). Alaska and Hawaii opted for statehood with the United States. Green- land and the Faroer have chosen autonomy under the Danish Crown. On numerous occasions, the Falklands and Gibraltar voted to remain British col- onies. In other cases too (e.g., Surinam, Cook Islands, Northern Mariana Is- lands), the population of a dependent territory has rejected independence. In Africa, most colonies have opted for independence as the goal of national self-determination, but not all have done so, and some have done so rather late. Until 1957, French Africa's leaders almost unanimously opposed inde- pendence and supported a federal or confederal French-African community as the proper goal of the right of self-determination. They wanted *liberté, fraternité,* and, especially, *égalité* for the Africans as French citizens within one political community. In 1958, this mood was confirmed in the plebiscite in which only Guinea opted for independence. In 1967, Djibouti still voted against independence. The island of Mayotte (which seceded from the Com- oros in 1975) and Réunion voted to become *départements d'outre-mer* and to "remain French." In the early 1970s, the majority of the Seychelles re- jected independence. Prime Minister James Mancham toured the African states in order to persuade them that the Seychelles should be allowed "to pursue their wish and remain British."[5] Later on, all twelve territories of French West Africa and French Equatorial Africa, Madagascar, Djibouti, and the Seychelles became independent. Even today both the UN and OAU re- fuse to interpret the decision of Mayotte and Réunion as a genuine act of self-determination. Their attitude is in line with the UN calls for the decol- onization of Gibraltar and the Falklands whose populations opted to remain colonized.

Some African colonies—such as British Somaliland and Italian Somalia, French Cameroun, and British Southern Cameroons—opted for unification. Others wished to join an independent state: the people of Spanish Morocco and Ifni joined Morocco in the 1950s and 1960s, and Eritrea's 1952 return to Ethiopia reflected the wish of at least the Tigrinya-speaking Christians. For independent states, national self-determination usually means guarding their independence against any foreign encroachments, but it may also mean choosing to forego separate sovereignty and join another indepen- dent state (as Zanzibar did in 1964). Usually, independence for the colony is the nationalists' first priority, but there are some rare examples where inde- pendence was granted even though it was not the majority's first choice. In 1960, the majority in Cyprus wanted unification with Greece and independence was the compromise solution between the conflicting demands of Greece and Turkey. In a similar way, Djibouti's independence was the only way to avoid war between Somalia and Ethiopia, although a really free vote without Ethiopian troops massing at the border might have tipped the balance toward integration with Somalia.

The goals of national selves within independent states vary from case to case. The goals may be independence (Biafra), integration with a neighboring state (the Somalis in the Ogaden and the NFD), or separation and establishment of a new state with parts of other states (the Bakongo in the 1950s). National selves may also opt for regional autonomy or federal statehood (the moderate Southern Sudanese and Eritreans and Nigerian minorities like the Tiv, Kanuri, Ijaw, and Efik in the 1960s). We may even count a millet-type cultural autonomy and a willed assimilation as proper goals of self-determination. Self-determination may very well mean self-limitation as long as it reflects the authentic will of a population. Other goals of self-determination may be international status or condominium and association, but in post-colonial Africa, these goals of self-determination were not pursued.

Very often, different goals are pursued by the same movement. Nationalists in the Southern Sudan, Eritrea, and Tigre have always included separatists, regional autonomists, or federalists. Somali nationalists in Ethiopia include irredentists (who want to join Somalia) and separatists who want independence for the Somali (and Abbo-Somali) areas of Ethiopia. The Issa-Somalis in Djibouti have shown the same ambivalence.

Another problem of self-determination is the "choice of choices": what alternatives are offered to the people in a plebiscite? Cyprus, for example, achieved self-determination in 1960, but it could only choose independence, not "*enosis*" (unification with Greece). In the "consultations" in West Irian in 1969, the Papuans were given the choice of integration or nonintegration with Indonesia. The independence option was never offered. In Africa, in at least three cases during the era of decolonization, the choice of choices was of prime importance. In 1960, the British Cameroons might have voted for independence rather than for amalgamation with Nigeria or Cameroun; but the UN supervised plebiscite offered only two options: fusion with the French Cameroun or integration with Nigeria. The same was true with British Togoland. The 1956 plebiscite in this trusteeship territory offered only two alternatives: integration with Ghana or continued British rule. Two other realistic options, unification with the former French Togo or independence, were ruled out.[6] In Djibouti, in all the plebiscites of the 1960s and 1970s, the option to join Somalia was never offered. The choice in 1958, 1967, and 1976 was between independence or a continuation of the colonial status quo. In this sense, Djibouti's options were almost the reverse of those presented to the British Cameroons and British Togoland. Most historical or ethnocultural selves were never offered any real choice in the first place. Their choice of choices was limited from the beginning between willingly acceding to independence within colonial boundaries, unwillingly resigning themselves to such boundaries, or taking up arms against the imposed postcolonial state. They never had the option of separating or of joining a neighboring state by a free vote.

Another question concerns the ways of ascertaining the wishes of a population. Plebiscites in a clearly delimited territory are one tool for achieving national self-determination. They were widely used in Europe, especially after the French Revolution (in Avignon, Comtat Venaissin, Savoy, Nice, Belgium, and the Rhine Valley), during the unification of Italy between 1848 and 1870, and after World War I (e.g., in Schleswig, Upper Silesia, and the Saar).

In Africa, plebiscites were widely used in the era of decolonization to determine if and when colonies should become independent. The 1958 plebiscite in the French colonies led to Guinea's independence and the rejection of independence by all the other territories. The Algerian plebiscite of 1962 ratified the Evian Agreements leading to independence. Djibouti voted against independence in the 1966 plebiscite and for independence in the 1976 plebiscite. The plebiscite on the Comoros in 1974 resulted in three islands voting for independence and one island, Mayotte, voting against. In 1976, the separatist self-determination of Mayotte was confirmed by yet another plebiscite.

Plebiscites have also determined whether countries should be amalgamated with a neighboring state. The 1922 "whites only" plebiscite determined that Rhodesia should not join South Africa. The 1956 plebiscite in British Togoland led to fusion with Ghana, while the British Cameroons plebiscite of 1961 resulted in the partition of the territory between Nigeria and Cameroon. In the current Western Sahara conflict, POLISARIO and its supporters strongly demand a plebiscite on the sovereignty issue. The Biafrans, Eritreans, Southern Sudanese, Somalis, Oromos, and other secessionists have all consented to recognize the plebiscite as the final arbiter in the secession and sovereignty issue. But plebiscites pose major problems, even if the definition of the self is agreed upon by all parties to the conflict. Who is to determine the fate of the self—the designated self (self-determination) or the whole of which the self is a part. In the Eritrean conflict, for example, the separatists insist on a plebiscite in Eritrea, while the Ethiopian government is only willing to concede that there is an Eritrean entity whose future will be determined by the "*entire* Ethiopian people."[7] What should be asked in a plebiscite? We have seen that the options given in Togoland, the Cameroons, and Djibouti were limited. Who should supervise the plebiscite? Should it be UN observers, as was the case in Togoland, the Cameroons, Equatorial Guinea, and the 1976 plebiscite in Djibouti (also attended by observers of the OAU and the Arab League), or should the administration of the plebiscite be trusted to the administering power (as was the case in French Africa in 1958, in Djibouti in 1966, and in the Comoros and Mayotte in 1974 and 1975)? Should the military and the administration of the occupying power stay during the plebiscite, as the French have always done in all their territories and as the Moroccans insist they will in the Western Sahara? Or should they be withdrawn and replaced by neutral forces, as Somali nationalists demanded in Djibouti and as SWAPO and POLISARIO demand in Namibia and the Western Sahara. Outside pressures, too, may make a plebiscite questionable, as did the concentration of Ethiopian and Somali troops on the borders of Djibouti during the 1966 plebiscite.

Another method of achieving self-determination is through representative institutions or institutions claiming to be representative. Independence was granted to many colonies on the basis of an official request by the territory's Legislative Council. Such was the case in Nigeria, Ghana, Sierra Leone, and the Sudan. The Legislative Council of British Somaliland, claiming to represent "the proper feeling in the country," decided to convene in April 1960 together with the parliament of Italian Somalia. This All Somali Conference decided on the unification of both territories "in due recognition of and for the expressed wishes of the Somali people wherever they are."[8] In the Western Sahara, for example, both Morocco and POLISARIO claimed the support of the *Djemaa*, the quasi parliament appointed in the early 1970s by the Spanish. Thus, both indirectly recognized the legitimacy and authority of that body with regard to self-determination for the Western Sahara. Morocco also emphasized that the chairman of the Djemaa, Khati Ould Said Ould al Joumani, had declared his allegiance to the Moroccan Crown "on behalf of the inhabitants and tribes of the Sahara."[9] Sometimes, nonindependent governments make the decision to ask for national self-determination and independence. Most Francophone governments did so in 1960. The elected Comoro government unilaterally declared independence in 1975. The decision to secede was taken by the regional government of Eastern Nigeria, the provincial government of Katanga, and the traditional governments of Sanwi, Barotse, and Buganda. Sometimes, the government's decision was authorized or initiated by a traditional parliament (Buganda's *Lukiko*) or a modern representative assembly (Biafra's Consultative Assembly). The government's determination was, in some cases, controversial in the seceding area (e.g., Katanga and Barotse), but in other cases, it enjoyed almost total support in the population (e.g., Biafra and Buganda).

Liberation movements themselves are often recognized as legitimate representatives of the national self. They are never elected to do so in any formal sense, but prove themselves to represent "the people" by waging an efficient political and military campaign. That holds true for SWAPO and the African National Congress (ANC) as it did earlier for the *Front de Libération*

Nationale (FLN), *Movimento Popular de Libertacao de Angola* (MPLA), *Frente de Libertacao de Mozambique* (FRELIMO), *Partido Africano da Independencia da Guine e Cabo Verde* (PAIGC), and the Patriotic Front in Zimbabwe. The same also holds for POLISARIO in the Western Sahara; the ELF and EPLF in Eritrea (the latter claiming to be "the *only* legitimate representative of the Eritrean people"); and the OLF, WSLF, and TPLF in Ethiopia.[10] In the Sudan, the Addis Ababa Accords of 1972 recognized the claim of the Southern Sudan Liberation Front (SSLF) and its military arm (*Anyanya*) to represent the Africans of the Southern Sudan. Some observers disputed the representativeness of some of these guerilla movements. Though there is no point in refuting their representativeness, it is important to emphasize that their recognition is based on popular support gained by armed struggle, not on elections and plebiscites.

Another way to effect self-determination is by sending investigation commissions. The Big Powers (in 1948) and the UN (in 1950) sent commissions of inquiry to Eritrea. In 1961, the UN did the same with regard to Ruanda-Urundi. Similar consultations were also conducted in disputed Asian territories (West Irian, Bahrein) or where the UN wanted first-hand information about the wishes of the people (Sabah, Sarawak). The British sent commissions of inquiry to the Kenyan NFD in 1962 and to Rhodesia in 1972 (the Pearce Commission) in order to consult the population of those territories. These commissions ascertained the wishes of the population through public hearings, meetings with delegations, and written petitions. The NFD Commission, for example, reported it had met 40,000 people in public hearings, heard 134 delegations, and received 106 petitions. The commission may come up with clear-cut evidence, as it did in the NFD case when it established that 87 percent of the population would opt for Somalia if they were given a free choice to attach themselves to either Kenya or Somalia. The commission may also come up with an ambivalent and divided opinion as in the Eritrean case when there was no conclusive evidence about the wishes of the Eritrean population. The divisions in the Eritrean population were reflected in the commission reports. The only option ruled out by the UN commissions on Eritrea was partition, but all the other options—independence, federation with Ethiopia and complete fusion with Ethiopia—found supporters in the investigation commissions. Ironically, while the clear-cut findings of the NFD Commission that the NFD population wanted to join Somalia did not lead to the separation of the NFD from Kenya and its fusion with Somalia, the UN decided to hand over Eritrea to Ethiopia in spite of the strong opposition by the Eritrean Muslims (and some of the urban Christians).

There are numerous other ways of achieving self-determination, but not all of them were tried in Africa. One is self-determination by petition, as done in Eupen-Malmédy in 1920. Another is self-determination by a ruler who supposedly reflects the wishes of the people. In 1947 in India, that was how the traditional rulers of the princely states decided whether to go to India or Pakistan. In Kashmir and Heyderabad, this procedure led to bloody conflicts.

"Nomadic self-determination," defined as "physically and collectively removing itself from the jurisdiction of the dominants' state and migrating to a new territorial home," is another variant of self-determination.[11] Migrations of this sort have been known from the dawn of history. In nineteenth century Africa, numerous peoples- –whether the African Ngoni or the Boer "trekkers"—moved for this reason from one territory to another. In post-colonial Africa, the Europeans of Algeria, Angola, Mozambique, and Zimbabwe, as well as millions of Eritreans, Somalis, Southern Sudanese, Tigrineans, and Saharwi "voted with their feet."

In most cases, the carrier of the struggle for national self-determination is the population, or part of the population, of the national self per se. But, sometimes, third parties have a decisive say. Such is also the case when national independence comes through military conquest by a third party (e.g., the Indian intervention in Bangladesh in 1971 or the British conquest of Ethiopia in 1941). In the case of Libya in 1949, the UN had a decisive say in Libya's becoming independent as "one whole." The decision on Eritrea's union with Ethiopia was, in final analysis, more a UN than an Eritrean decision. In many of the irredentist cases the major champion of national self-determination is not the population involved but the neighboring state. Examples are Somalia and the Ogaden and NFD, Morocco and the Western Sahara, Togo and the Victoria Region of Ghana, Zaire and Cabinda, or Lesotho and the Sotho area of South Africa.

An important problem in ascertaining the wishes of the self is how to make the affected people aware that their votes or opinions may be crucial to their futures. There are indications that in Togoland and the Cameroons this was not always done.

It is possible to differentiate between self-determination "from below" by elections, plebiscites, or a mass-based guerilla movement and "self-determination from above" by rulers, oligarchies, nonrepresentative parliaments and elitist movements. One may also start a guerilla war with a small band from above and end up with mass support from below. How many people have to support self-determination to be considered true representatives of the popular will? There is no ready-made formula or answer. Demands for national self-determination may often be countered by arguing that the proponents of self-determination are an unrepresentative minority. The colonial governments argued that way, but the Ethiopian, Nigerian, and Sudanese governments did the same, using the same words with the same intentions.

5

THE RIGHT OF SECESSION

Plainly, the central idea of secession is the essence of anarchy.
Abraham Lincoln, 1861[1]

The history of national self-determination is a history of the making of nations and the breaking of states.
Alfred Cobban, 1944[2]

The 20th century bias against political divorce, that is secession, is just as strong as the 19th century bias against marital divorce.
Samuel Huntington, 1979[3]

Self-determination does not mean secession, nor does it mean unity for the sake of unity.
Tigre People's Liberation Front, 1975[4]

The desire for separation always springs from the recognition that a certain socio-economic and cultural community is badly governed by the state to which it belongs.
Joseph Tubiana, 1980[5]

Liberal political philosophy required that secession be permitted if it is effectively desired by a territorially concentrated group within a state and is morally and practically possible.
Harry Beran, 1984[6]

In the twentieth century, many nations gained independence through separatist self-determination (e.g., Poland, Norway, Ireland, Iceland, Czechoslovakia, Panama, Pakistan, and Bangladesh), while many more movements for separation were defeated by the power of the state (e.g., Ukrainian, Georgian, Croat, Basque, Kurdish, Sikh, and Tibetan).

It has always been disputed whether the principle of self-determination contains the right of secession. In the early twentieth century, there was an interesting debate on this issue in the socialist movement. Lenin's pre-1917 writings strongly supported the right of secession,[7] while Karl Renner, Otto Bauer, and Rosa Luxemburg argued for national "internal self-determination" *within* existing states.[8] For Lenin, self-determination could not have any other meaning besides "political self-determination, political independence, the formation of a national state."[9] Here lies the ideological root for the constitutional peculiarity of the USSR which, in its 1924, 1936, and 1977 constitutions, at least pays lip service to the right of each Union Republic "to freely secede from the USSR."[10] The debate, waged in Eastern Europe in the nineteenth and twentieth centuries, is relevant to anyone interested in postcolonial Africa because the complex ethnic map of Eastern Europe was comparable to the situation in black Africa.

Jefferson and Lincoln were in favor of the fullest democracy but opposed secession by self-determination. Many scholars argue that even Woodrow Wilson opposed separatist self-determination and that his Wilsonian principles were only intended to democratize the multinational states and to prevent territorial changes without the consent of the population involved. European *statist* nationalists opposed *ethnic* separatism, arguing that the national self which they defined as the nation-state is an indivisible organism. Documents published about the San Francisco Conference in 1945 reveal that those who drafted the UN Charter, which declares "the right of all peoples to self-determination," did not support secession by self-determination. There was an understanding that the right to self-determination conformed to the purposes of the charter "only insofar as it implied the right of self-government of peoples and *not* the right of secession."[11] The 1960 UN Declaration on the Granting of Independence to Colonial Countries talked about "the right of self-determination of all peoples," but regarded it as incompatible with the UN Charter to discuss "any attempt aimed at the partial or total disruption of the national unity and territorial integrity of a country."[12] The 1970 UN Declaration on Friendly Relations and Cooperation among States says that "the territorial integrity and political independence of every state is indivisible" and that nothing should be done "to dismember or impair, totally or in part, the territorial integrity and political unity of sovereign and independent states."[13]

"Maximalist self-determination," which includes the right of secession, is opposed by the statists and supporters of the status quo as undermining international order and stability by legitimizing revisionism in international politics. Secession is sometimes also rejected because it may lead to "trapped minorities" in relatively homogenous states and "stranded majorities," when wealthy regions secede in order not to share their wealth with less fortunate regions.[14] Another argument against separatism through national self-determination is that "no truly objective criteria exist for establishing the identity or limits of the nation, or even for ascertaining unambiguously the national will." For this very reason, "it is impossible to distinguish in general terms between those secessionist or irredentist movements whose rebellions against the established order are justified and those that are not."[15]

There is no question that the doctrine of states' rights has become a central principle of the international legal order,[16] but it remains equally true that "nationalists have been destroyers of states as often as they have been associated with the construction of states."[17] Supporters of the right of secession argue that the right of national determination without the right of secession is like democracy without elections. They believe that the democratic values which underlie the right of self-determination contain the right of a people to withdraw from a state if they wish to do so, particularly if they have faced discrimination and oppression in the state from which they want to secede. Arend Lijphart would argue that in plural societies where assimilation is resisted and elite cooperation ("consociationalism") is impossible because of historical enmity, partition or separation become the only viable alternatives.[18] The right of secession is seen as a variant of the right of self-defense—you defend yourself by seceding from an oppressive system. Supporters of the right of secession from an oppressive system can convincingly mobilize traditional democratic principles like the social contract, the consent of the governed, and the right of rebellion. Representative of this attitude is Connor Cruise O'Brien who attacked the "sovereign legitimism, which treats the boundaries as more sacrosanct than the lives of stigmatized peoples."[19] Many supporters of the right of secession concede that not *all* groups can be granted the right of secession. They would not deny that the separatist self-determination of Czechoslovakia, Poland, Finland, Hungary, the Baltic States, and Ireland in post-World War I Europe has left many minorities in the newly created nation-states, but they would argue that it makes a difference whether sixty or twenty million people regard themselves as oppressed minorities. Usually, the supporters of the right of secession will limit this right to cases where there are "compelling reasons" to secede. Nevertheless, they totally reject the concept of the indivisibility of nations and the notion that the integrity of the state is an absolute value. There can be compelling reasons for secession such as if the physical survival or the cultural autonomy of a nation is threatened, or if a population would feel economically excluded and permanently deprived. Michael Walzer would go further and grant the right of secession to any distinct community whose fight for separation enjoys overwhelming popular support.[20] There are even some scholars who regard all talk about anarchy and instability brought about by the right of secession as cynical rationalization of statist power interests.[21]

It is unclear whether self-determination and the right of secession are two sides of the same coin or different principles. Many African leaders attempt to reconcile the right of national self-determination with an insistent, though not always consistent, rejection of the right of secession. The African "establishment approach," as represented by the OAU in its charter and resolutions and by most African governments, is strongly statist-conservative and opposed to secession. The OAU Charter, which stresses "territorial integrity," and the OAU Cairo Resolution, which sanctifies the postcolonial boundaries, truly reflect this status quo ideology.

National self-determination is often perceived as a positive principle, while separatism has the reputation for being negative and disruptive. For this very reason, that which is positive national self-determination for one party frequently becomes negative separatism for the other. During the Algerian War, for example, the supporters of *"Algerie française"* called the Algerian nationalists separatists, while the FLN guerillas regarded themselves as freedom fighters fighting for national self-determination and liberation. They did not perceive themselves as separatists because they did not regard Algeria as an integral part of France. While the Ethiopian governments attack the Somali separatists, the Somali liberation songs say "let us reject separatism and be under one house."[22] For the Ethiopians, separatism means the disintegration of the *state,* for the Somalis it means the partition of their *nation.*

One way to support self-determination but oppose secession is simply to deny the logical connection between the two. Thus, the Kenya delegation to the Addis Ababa Summit of the African Heads of State in May 1963 distributed a pamphlet which said that "the principle of self-determination has no relevance where the issue is territorial disintegration."[23] Others go so far as to see in secession a distortion or even a negation of the principle of national self-determination. The former president of Cameroun Ahmadu Ahidjo warned that an imprudent interpretation of self-determination would lead to "more Biafras" and to the disintegration of the African state system.[24] The former Senegalese Prime Minister Mahmadu Dia saw in secession a "negation" of the principle of self-determination because it destroys the "national reality."[25]

Another way open to those seeking to reconcile self-determination and opposition to secession is the adoption of nomadic self-determination. Nomadic self-determination means that people determine their destiny by moving to where they would like to live. Zionism—both Jewish and black— has been a form of nomadic self-determination. Where people feel unfree and suppressed and leave of their own volition, they exercise the right of nomadic self-determination. Traditional Africa, which did not know European ideas of self-determination, knew very well the practice of nomadic self-determination. In postcolonial Africa, leaders have returned to this traditional device in order to make self-determination and indivisibility compatible. The Kenyans publicly declared "if anyone wishes to exercise the right of self-determination, let him exercise that right by moving out of the country if necessary but not seek to balkanize Africa any further under the guise of so-called self-determination." The Kenyans explained that for the Kenya Somalis, "the only way they can legally exercise their right of self-determination" is by crossing the border to Somalia. Jomo Kenyatta was even more blunt suggesting that the Somalis could "pack up their camels and go to Somalia" if they don't want "to integrate with the rest of the Africans" in Kenya.[26] Ethiopian leaders have voiced a similar determination to hold on to the Ogaden, even if the Ogaden Somalis leave (as a matter of fact, since 1977, hundreds of thousands of Ogadenees have exercised nomadic self-determination by fleeing to Somalia).[27]

During the Nigeria-Biafra war, all major Nigerian leaders (Gowon, Awolowo, Enahoro) stressed their support for the right of self-determination of all Nigerian nationalities but emphasized their opposition to the right of secession.[28] Prior to 1967, that was also the position of the Biafran leaders (Ojukwu, Okpara, Azikiwe).[29] When the Nigerian leaders talked about the right to national self-determination, what they came to mean was the right of nationalities to form federal states *within* Nigeria. Nigeria's Foreign Minister during the war, Okoi Arikpo, compared the "sacred" right of national self-determination of the Ibos "*in* the overall national context of Nigeria" to the rights of Alsace-Lorraine and Brittany to autonomy within France.[30] Like the Nigerians, most African leaders oppose secession but accept the principle of national self-determination as part of a cherished value system which includes democracy, the sovereignty of the people, equality, and socialism.[31] It is difficult for them to reject outright the principle of self-determination. Self-determination thus has to be interpreted in such a way that it excludes the possibility of secession.

Another more practical way to avoid the intellectual embarrassment of opposing self-determination is to deny that the demand for secession is raised in the name of the majority and therefore to oppose the demand as a distortion of true self-determination. In the case of Katanga, it was argued that the separatist demand was not "autodétérmination authentique decidée par la majorité du peuple" was at least partially true.[32] (In the May 1960 national elections, the secessionist CONAKAT scored 32.07 percent of the votes, while the antisecessionist Cartel got 33.67 percent of the vote. In the provincial parliament, the CONAKAT majority was very narrow.) On the other hand, Kenyatta's assertion that in the NFD, "it is only a small section who wants to secede,"[33] and that the Somali leaders who demanded secession were "unrepresentative,"[34] was wholly unconvincing. Emperor Haile Selassie and his Marxist successor, Mengistu Haile Mariam, argued that the people in Eritrea did not want secession, that the secessionists were a minority incited by foreign powers. In the case of the Ibos, there is hardly any disagreement among the experts of what the overwhelming majority thought and felt between 1967 and 1970. The Nigerian leaders simply disregarded the evidence and argued that the Ibo "masses" supported Nigeria and opposed secession,[35] that those masses lived in a separatist state built on tyranny from which they wanted to escape,[36] that Ibo self-determination was a hoax,[37] and that the decision to secede was taken by a clique without any mandate from the people.[38] These statements reflect the ideological dilemma of those African leaders who oppose secession. The curious thing about the argument that the majority in Biafra, Katanga, Eritrea, or the NFD were against secession is that it indirectly recognized their right to self-determination and secession. This argument is very different from that which denies Biafra, Katanga, Eritrea, or the NFD the right to be the relevant self for self-determination. While the definition of the whole state as the only appropriate unit for self-determination is a principled rejection of secession, the argument by state leaders that the true majority in the seceding group is anti-secessionist could easily boomerang if popular support for the secessionists became very visible. It is a reflex defense against the allegation that Ibos, Katangese, Eritreans, or Kenya Somalis have been denied the right of secession. Nevertheless, such defensive arguments reflect an uneasiness about the reconcilability of support for self-determination and opposition to secession.

Emerson wrote that "the sword of self-determination is sharp when severing the colony from its metropole. However, its reverse side is blunt and unavailable when minorities within the former colonies seek either their own independence or union with more desirable brothers across the frontier."[39] African leaders who oppose secession by self-determination do so without rejecting the principle of the right of national self-determination.

We have seen that African leaders try to reconcile acceptance of the right of self-determination with opposition to the right of secession. Their arguments resemble those used by opponents of secession in Europe in the nineteenth and twentieth centuries. Both have argued that one may be loyal to the ideas of liberty, democracy, and self-determination without being compelled to recognize the right of secession. In both Europe and Africa, some were sincere and some were cynical about the possibility of reconciling self-determination and opposition to secession, but self-determination was too legitimate a value to be openly challenged.

As in Europe, *some* African leaders have come to the conclusion that the right to national self-determination may very well mean or include the right of secession. A major argument for secession is based on the notion that a people who did not consent to be included in a particular state has the moral right to decide by itself and for itself whether it wants to stay within the imposed colonial boundaries. Morocco's UN delegate once raised the rhetorical question of how the condemnation of the partition of Africa could be reconciled with its sanctification which leads to opposition to any boundary revisions and, in this way, forces some peoples to reside in states in which they do not wish to live.[40] Another related rationale for secession is the denial of a share in government to a particular group. Albert Hirshman suggests the alternatives of "voice" and "exit" for groups in a state. Those who have no voice may very well insist on their right for exit.[41] Mazrui puts the problem even more bluntly. He sees the postcolonial African states as based on "European agreement from without" and not on "African agreement from within." He knows that African states based on the consent of the governed may mean independent states for Ibos, Balubas, Ewes, and Touaregs. "'Government by the Baluba': isn't that the most meaningful expression of government by the people if we accept Burke's insistence on common agreement as a defining characteristic of a people?"[42] In 1958, the first All African Peoples' Conference linked the issue of border changes to self-determination. It called on the independent states of Africa "to support permanent solutions [to the problem of artificial boundaries] founded upon the true wishes of the people." The Southern Sudanese insist that their right to national self-determination and secession is moral and justified because "they have never been consulted in a free referendum to decide to be part of the North."[43] The Southern Sudanese Dunstan Wai insists that the fate of the Southern Sudanese Africans to be part of independent Sudan was sealed by Egyptians, Northern Sudanese Arabs, and the British.[44] This is "other determination," not self-determination. From 1960 to the present, all Somali leaders (Osman, Hussein, Shermarke, Egal, Barré) have demanded the right of self-determination and secession for the Somalis in Kenya, Ethiopia, and Djibouti.[45] For pragmatic reasons, they did not always pursue their goal actively, but they never compromised on the principle of a Greater Somalia for all Somalis. The Somali leaders refuse to regard their conflicts with their neighbors as "boundary disputes" resulting from differing interpretations of colonial treaties. They insist that their demands are consistent with the universal principle of national self-determination. The following quotation is representative of the Somali view that the demand for a Greater Somalia is based on the principle of national self-determination and not on refined legalistic arguments about minor clauses in an international treaty: "The case of the Somali people in the occupied territories is not that of a boundary. It is the case of independence and self-determination."[46] The Biafran struggle was also fought in the name of self-determination. The secession began with the call of Ibo students at Nsukka University and Ibo professors at Ibadan University to grant the Ibos the right of national self-determination.[47] Ojukwu's words resembled the traditional European and American terminology about self-determination for oppressed nations. Ojukwu talked about his people being "born free," people's "inalienable rights,"[48] "people's will,"[49] and the "inalienable rights to self-determination"[50] and "self-preservation."[51]

Ojukwu insisted that Eastern Nigerians possessed the right of national self-determination and secession, although he still believed in 1966 that there was no need to use this right.[52] Like Lenin, Ojukwu made the distinction between the right of secession, which stands in general, and the desirability of secession, which differs from case to case. In the early 1960s, all major Nigerian leaders supported the right of secession of Hausas, Yorubas, and Ibos. The opposition to secession was far weaker at that time than in the 1970s and 1980s after the Biafran trauma.

Ahmadu Bello was in favor of a Northern secession in the 1950s, and insisted that the fate of the North ought to be in Northern hands.[53] In fact, in the 1950s and 1960s the North was on the verge of secession four times.[54] In 1950, the Northern Emirs threatened to secede if the North did not receive at least 50 percent of the seats in parliament. In 1953, the Northern House of Assembly and the Northern House of Chiefs passed resolutions in favor of secession should the South not agree to delay independence. At that point, Bello talked about the creation of Nigeria as the "mistake of 1914." Again, in 1960, the North made it clear that a Southern NCNC-AG (Action Group) coalition would lead to the breakup of the Federation. Finally, the July 1966 coup was instigated under the motto "*a raba a ware*" (let us secede), and only a coup within the coup prevented the secession of the North.

In his autobiography, Awolowo stressed the right of self-determination of all Nigerian peoples. He made it clear that he did not exclude the right of secession:

> When Britain brought together all the ethnic groups in Nigeria, she had done so in the pursuit of her national interest . . . without the consent of the people . . . On the eve of her surrender of sovereignty to them, therefore, she owes it as a duty to them to give them all the right to self-determination.[55]

Awolowo insisted that the Nigerian tribes were in fact nations in no way different from the English, Scots, and Welshmen. He demanded that the Ibos, Yorubas, and Hausas be granted the right of national self-determination. He explained that Wales was part of Britain because the people of Wales continued to support the association with England. His message was clear: the Yorubas may continue their association with the other nations of Nigeria, but they also have the right not to do so. Like the Welshmen, the Yorubas have the right of national self-determination because they are recognized as a national self. Like the North, the West threatened more than once with secession in the 1950s and 1960s. A few months before the Biafran War,

Awolowo still defined the Northern troops in the West as an "army of occupation" and threatened with the secession of the West if the East should secede.[56]

Azikiwe, who denied the legitimacy of secession in the 1950s and early 1960s, later came to support the Biafran side by insisting on "the natural and inalienable right of the Ibos and fellow Easterners to self-determination."[57] Even in the prewar period, Azikiwe's opposition to separatism lacked consistency. Thus, at the end of the colonial period, he recognized "the right of the North to secede," although he personally did not advocate a Northern secession.[58] As early as 1964, Azikiwe, then still President of Nigeria, suggested that "we should separate in peace and not in pieces." Eastern Nigeria's Prime Minister Michael Okpara then pushed for secession.

A few months before the declaration of Biafra's independence, *all* major political groupings in Nigeria declared their support for the right of secession of the four major Nigerian regions. And in the Ad Hoc Constitutional Conference of September 1966, all regional delegations recognized the right of secession. The Northern representative even insisted that the right be regarded as "absolute" and "unilateral," and in fact advocated the immediate creation of four independent states in Nigeria which would cooperate in a similar way as Kenya, Uganda, and Tanzania cooperated in the East African Common Services Organization.[59] The West pushed for the right of unilateral secession and suggested the Commonwealth of Nations as an alternative model for cooperation; the East talked about a confederal arrangement which would have granted the four regions almost complete independence.[60]

The African states which granted full diplomatic recognition to Biafra (Tanzania, Zambia, Gabon, Ivory Coast) did it in the name of national self-determination and consent of the governed. The case of Tanzania is particularly revealing, for Julius Nyerere was the author of the OAU Cairo Resolution of 1964, which solemnly declared its support for existing boundaries and the territorial integrity of the postcolonial states. Separatists and their supporters were often accused of being "stooges of colonialism," but Nyerere's support for Biafra was different, for nobody could deny his African-nationalist credentials.

Separatism everywhere has been justified as a legitimate response to oppression. Such was the case in Ireland, Poland, the American Colonies, colonial Africa, Kurdistan, and Bangladesh. One can argue quite logically that a group would not "wish to go through the very considerable trouble of disrupting the unity of a state" if it is not oppressed in one way or another.[61] The Tigrinean nationalists of the TPLF clearly defined oppression as explaining and justifying secession: "If there is a democratic political atmosphere, self-determination means the creation of integrated nations . . . If the existing national oppression continues or is aggravated, then it means the birth of an independent Tigray."[62] The Southern Sudanese also regarded their war of secession as a war for self-preservation and safety and against genocide and "cultural-assimilationist conquest."[63] Another example of separatism as a response to persecution and slaughter is the case of South Kasai. Albert Kalonji explained the independence of South Kasai as the Balubas' reaction to their oppression by the Lulua of Northern Kasai. The South Kasai declaration of independence stated that "given the profound hatred and the irreducible spirit of vengeance which are the irremedial consequence of eleven months of arson, pillaging, massacres, mutilations, hatred and vengeance . . . the division of Kasai is necessary at any cost."[64]

A basic tenet in Nyerere's defense of Biafra was the basic right to life of every people. Nyerere accused Gowon's government of committing genocide by initiating pogroms against the Ibos before the war, and later, by imposing on Biafra's population a hunger blockade.[65] Nyerere insisted that in the case of Biafra, the right to exist meant the right to break away from the Federation of Nigeria. Generally, peoples who fight for national self-determination and independence do it in the name of the right to exist, whether physically or culturally. Therefore, Nyerere's argument did not constitute a special case relating to a unique situation. Rather, it was the traditional defense of secession by self-determination in a context which was as common as separatism in recent history:

> When the machinery of the state and the powers of the government are turned against a whole group of the society on the grounds of racial, tribal or religious prejudice, then the victims have the right to take back the powers they have surrendered and to defend themselves . . . the people have the right to create another instrument for their protection; in other words, to create another state.[66]

> "Surely when a whole people is rejected by the majority of the state in which they live, they must have the right to live under a different government which does secure their existence."[67]

Nyerere insisted that after the horrors which occurred in Northern Nigeria, the Ibos could not be forced to live in a united Nigeria. Basing his case on classical Western political philosophy, and thus echoing Burke, Locke and Jefferson, Nyerere emphasized the legitimacy of the right of secession in the name of self-determination: "What Tanzania's action does do is to warn that unless governments are based on consent of the governed, they will not enjoy the loyalty of the governed."[68] Nyerere's intellectual defense of Biafra was even more blunt and heretical with respect to Africa's dominant status quo ideology than Ojukwu's defense of Biafra's secession. While Ojukwu frequently attempted to "apologize" for secession by stressing that there was no other choice for the Ibos because they were "rejected" and "pushed out" and threatened with "genocide," Nyerere's party organ ridiculed the whole "hysteria about the evil of secession"[69] and demanded that the right to secede be made a basic constitutional right. "For honest people secessions are not always evil or reprehensible. Honest people will ask if the constitution of a political entity allows parties to the system to get out."[70] Nyerere's attitude towards Biafra is significant because it indicates that under crisis conditions, the status quo ideology may easily collapse. The absence of any known opposition inside Tanzania to Nyerere's stand on Biafra shows how easily a major ideological *volte face* on the issue of self-determination and secession can be accomplished. There is hardly any evidence that Nyerere lost prestige in black Africa since his heretical and dramatic recognition of Biafra. All indicators showed an actual rise in his popularity, and his establishment as one of the few African leaders respected throughout the continent.

The Western values of humanism, democracy, and liberalism, and their acceptance and internalization by parts of the new African elite, provide a fertile ground for the legitimation of secession in specific situations in the name of inalienable rights, self-determination, consent of the governed, popular will, group-autonomy, the right to self-preservation, and the right to equality. The whole Tanzanian argument during the Nigeria-Biafra war rested on this philosophical heritage.

Nyerere's use of the principle of national self-determination to explain his sympathetic attitude towards Biafra was imitated by other African supporters of the Biafran secession. Félix Houphouët-Boigny saw in the phenomenon of Biafra "la détermination d'un peuple de vivre une vie indépendente."[71] Houphouët also referred to the Western concept of the state as a contract when he said that "unity is the fruit of the common will to live together. It should not be imposed by force by one group upon another . . . unity is for the living and not for the dead."[72] The Gabonese recognition of Biafra was also based on the "right to self-determination" and the right to exist.[73] Zambia's Kenneth Kaunda stressed the need for "consent of all the parties concerned," a consent which was absent in Nigeria in 1968.[74] Even heads of state who did not accord full diplomatic recognition to Biafra hinted that secession might be legitimate in the face of harsh oppression. Dahomey's president, Emile Zinsou, ridiculed the "boundaries of colonization" which were "so well made as to be irreversible," and "in respect of them," thousands had to die.[75] Leopold Senghor sharply criticized the "genocide" in Biafra and the Southern Sudan, and even Tunisia's Habib Bourgiba attacked Nigeria's "murderous and genocidal struggle."[76] Biafra's separatism was widely perceived in Africa as a justified response to the mass slaughter of the Ibos and other Easterners in Northern Nigeria in July and

September 1966. Biafra was diplomatically recognized by only four African states, but other African governments also sympathized with the separatists, demonstrated neutrality, or offered only lukewarm opposition (e.g., Kenya, Liberia, Ethiopia, Zaire, Ghana, Senegal, Dahomey, Tunisia, Uganda, Rwanda, Burundi, Sierra Leone, Botswana).[77] Public opinion in many of the predominantly Christian countries was strongly pro-Biafran (Ghana is a good example). It is not true that there was an African consensus against Biafra's secession. And it is off the mark to argue that Biafra's separatist illegitimacy brought about its military defeat. It is rather the other way around: Biafra's military collapse prevented it from gaining wide legitimacy. Here lies the essential difference between Bangladesh's success and Biafra's failure. The Bangladeshis defeated the Pakistanis with the help of the Indian army. Biafra had no India and was defeated.

In general, in spite of the OAU Charter, the Cairo Resolution, and the myth of a consistent African consensus against separatism, things look very different in reality. Katanga enjoyed the support of Congo-Brazzaville and the Malagasy Republic, and other members of the Brazzaville bloc were lukewarm in their opposition to Katanga's secession.[78] The Eritrean secessionists enjoyed strong support in the North African Arab countries and, by 1981, Mauritania, the Ivory Coast, Togo, Benin, Niger, Somalia, Mozambique, and the Malagasy Republic also had come out in support of the Eritrean right to self-determination. The Southern Sudanese separatists could not have operated without at least intermittent support from Ethiopia, Zaire, and Uganda. Greater Somalia was popular with the Arab and Muslim states and even Nkrumah declared (together with Somali president Osman) that he "recognized the imperative need to remove the existing frontiers artificially demarcated by the colonialists without respect for ethnic, cultural and economic links."[79] Nkrumah also actively supported the Agni separatists of MOLISAN (*Mouvement Libération Sanwi*) and talked about the Southern Sudanese freedom fighters. In the 1970s, Cabinda's separatism enjoyed strong support in Zaire and the Congo. President Mobutu supported the Louis Ranque Franque faction of FLEC, while President Ngouabi was the patron of the N'zita Henriques Tiago faction. But both declared that Cabinda is not part of Angola. Zaire prohibited the FNLA from operating in Cabinda and, in November 1975, unsuccessfully invaded the enclave, while the People's Republic of the Congo declared its opposition to a solution "imposed by force" by the MPLA. For a while, Amin's Uganda also supported Cabindan separatism.[80] The Ewe separatists of TOLIMO (Togoland Liberation Movement) in Ghana also received support from African states (e.g., the Ivory Coast, Libya and Guinea) in the 1970s.[81] Even in revolutionary Ethiopia, some of the political organizations (e.g., Meison and Echaat) supported the right of secession in the late 1970s.[82] While the OAU and most governments certainly reject the right of secession, the degree of rejection is often vastly exaggerated.

All the secessionists claim they struggle for national self-determination and the right of secession. All their opponents deny that the right of national self-determination includes the right of secession. Both sides simply believe in two different versions of national self-determination. In that sense, things are not that much different in Africa from what they were in Central and Eastern Europe in the last century.

WHAT IS "COLONIAL"?

*The sea, O the sea "a gradh-gheal mo chroi." Long may it roll between Eng-
land and me. God help the poor Scotsmen, they'll never be free. But we are
surrounded by water.*

Traditional Irish Song[1]

The problem of the 20th century is the problem of the colour line.

W.E.B. DuBois, 1919[2]

The white imperialist must not be replaced by the black.

Northern People's Party, The Gold Coast, 1954[3]

*Oppression of white men by white men is viewed by many Asians and Afri-
cans as different and perhaps less deplorable than the oppression of colored men by white men.*

Ivo D. Duchacek, 1975[4]

*Whether to view the Eritrean question as a colonial question or whether to
reject this view is not an academic question but of principal significance.*

Ethiopian Students Union of North America, 1976[5]

In the eyes of most African leaders, national self-determination means
emancipation from *colonial* rule. In the UN and OAU, there was strong support for limiting the right of national self-determination to colonial territories. Ronen reminds us that Africa's multiethnic states, which were
created as political entities by the European powers, are not genuine nations.[6] That means that *national* self-determination was granted to units
which hardly could claim to be national. The question of "what is colonial"
had to be answered for those whose support for self-determination was limited to colonial cases.

In general, most Afro-Asians define "colonial" according to what Emerson called the "salt water theory of colonialism."[7] According to this popular theory a colony has to be a territory separated from a mother country by salt waters. Han-Chinese domination of Tibetans, Uighurs, Mongols, and Koreans would, according to this definition, not count as colonial because there are no separating salt waters. Even Russia's Asian territories populated by Asian peoples and dominated by European ethnic Russians do not qualify as colonies because there is no salt water between them and Russia proper. This situation led British Prime Minister Lord Hume to complain bitterly "that there is one rule for the British Empire and another for the Russian Empire."[8] In Africa, only the *overseas* possessions of the British, French, Belgians, Portuguese, Spanish, Italians, and Germans would have counted as true colonies. That means that Amhara rule in the Somali-inhabited Ogaden, Arab domination of the Southern Sudan, Shona government in Zimbabwe, or Hausa-Fulani predominance in the whole of Nigeria would not have been regarded as colonial, however foreign, discriminatory, or oppressive it may have been.

The salt water theory gradually became the official UN point of view. Thus, while the UN Charter defined colonies (or "non self-governing territories") as "territories whose peoples have not yet attained a full measure of self-government,"[9] twenty-five years later, the UN defined a colony as "*geographically separate* and distinct ethnically and/or culturally from the country administering it."[10] The salt water theory was widely accepted in Africa and truly reflected the OAU position. It explains the African establishment position that national self-determination should only be supported in European overseas colonies. This position denies the legitimacy of the right to national self-determination if applied to ethnic groups or regions *within* independent states in the Third World. Self-determination is supported for the Gold Coast Colony but not for Ashantiland, for the Kenya Colony but not for the Luo Country, for Colonial Nigeria but not for Iboland.

The dominant Third World position on colonialism goes even further than the salt water theory. It refuses self-determination to European settled colonies even if they are beyond salt waters. According to the salt water theory, the largely European population of Gibraltar and the Falklands should have been granted the right to self-determination, but the UN majority refused to do so. The cases of UDI-Rhodesia and South Africa were different because they did not have a European majority, but nevertheless, they had no motherland and were overseas and thus, according to Emerson's theory, could have been granted the right to anticolonial self-determination.

According to a strict application of the salt water theory, South African rule in Namibia is not colonial, while Fang rule in Fernando Poo or Comorian claims to Mayotte could be termed colonial. These examples show that, in addition to the salt water theory, we have to introduce a racial dimension to understand why there was no question that the UN and the OAU grant the right of national self-determination to the *European* population of Algeria and Rhodesia in the past or to the Afrikaners of South Africa or the Europeans of Réunion today. Mazrui is on the right track in arguing that for most Third World governments, anticolonial self-determination means pigmentational self-determination—the liberation of colored peoples from white-European rule.[11] Kedourie's observation that colonial rule is European and not just racial rule is even more exact.[12] It explains why Arab domination of black Africans in the Sudan and Mauritania is in general not perceived as colonial rule. Although not black, the Arabs are accepted as native Africans, and Arab domination of Dinkaland or Moorish rule over the Toucouleur in Mauritania is thus not perceived as qualitatively different from Hausa-Fulani dominance in Nigeria or Kikuyu dominance in Kenya. A combination of Emerson's salt water theory, Mazrui's pigmentational logic, and Kedourie's definition of colonial rule enables us to understand why for most African governments anticolonial self-determination did not apply to the Biafrans, Southern Sudanese, Katangese, Ogaden and NFD Somalis, Cabindans, Lozi, Agni, Saharwi, and Touareg in Mali and Niger who revolted against governments which were neither overseas nor European. The position of the Third World was best represented by a joint declaration of Emperor Haile Selassie and the President of India: "The principle of self-determination should apply only to colonial territories which have not yet attained their independence and are not parts of sovereign and independent states."[13] According to this formula, self-determination does not apply to territories annexed by a Third World state—it does not apply to Goa or Kashmir, Eritrea or the Ogaden. Another example is an official Kenyan declaration that "the principle of self-determination only has relevance where foreign domination is the issue," and it is clear that for the Kenyans, "foreign" equals "European."[14] By that definition, Kenyan rule in the Somali areas is *not* foreign. The dominant Third World definition of colonialism explains why there is no general support for POLISARIO in the Western Sahara and the ELF and EPLF in Eritrea, even though both territories were former colonies. In both cases, the struggle is for liberation from non-European native rule (Moroccan and Ethiopian), and the territories cannot be defined by the salt water theory as colonial. The fact that the UN acquiesced to the transfer of colonial territories to Indonesia, India, China, Benin, and Morocco without insisting on plebiscites to ascertain the wishes of the populations involved proves that, for much of the world's establishment, national self-determination is simply equivalent to termination of European rule. This is the dominant point of view, although it may not have been popular in Hong Kong and Macao, Goa and Timor, West Irian and Gibraltar, the Western Sahara and the Ogaden, Eritrea and Iboland, Lundaland and Southern Sudan, and Northern Mali and Southern Mauritania.

As long as African nationalism was principally anticolonialism directed against white-European rule in European-controlled colonies, there was a consensus on what was meant by national self-determination. Very soon after independence, the secessionists redefined colonialism by rejecting the salt water fallacy and the pigmentational definition of self-determination.

Again and again, Somali leaders talk about colonial rule in the Haud, Ogaden, and the NFD. Their ethnic-cultural nationalism leads them to speak about Amhara and Kikuyu—rather than Ethiopian or Kenyan—colonialism.[15] The religious component was sometimes stressed as when Sheikh Farah, the minister of Somali affairs, spoke about the Somalis "still under the yoke of the worst Christian imperialism."[16] The Somalis call their "brothers" across the border in the "occupied territories" the "colonized Somalis."[17] The Somali leaders attempt to legitimize the idea of a Greater Somalia by equating their demand for self-determination with anticolonial self-determination. They stress their view that colonial rule cannot be defined as rule by whites: "Why does the world think only in terms of white colonialism? There is black imperialism too. Why should Somalis remain under Amhara or Kikuyu masters any more than Italian or British ones?"[18] The Somali Constitution of 1973 pledges "liberation of Somali territories under colonial oppression."[19] The Somalis also declare that the OAU principle regarding the sanctity of boundaries cannot apply to a colonial power. For them, Ethiopia (and to a lesser degree, Kenya) is a colonial power *par excellence*, and the right of the Ogadenees to self-determination is in no way different from what was the recognized right of the Angolans and Mozambiquans to emancipation from Portuguese rule.

The Oromos also apply the colonial terminology to Amhara-ruled Ethiopia. The OLF talks about its opposition to Amhara colonialization, about the colonial regime in Addis Ababa, and the determination of the OLF to wage an anticolonial struggle.[20] The same is true for the Eritrean separatists. The National Democratic Programme of the EPLF constantly refers to "Ethiopian colonialism," "colonial Ethiopia," the Ethiopian "colonial aggression," and the Ethiopian "colonial army."[21] For Bereket Habte Selassie, the Eritreans are a "colonized people engaged in the struggle for self-determination and independence from colonial rule." He concludes that the "Eritrean struggle involves a colonial question and not one of secession."[22]

It is interesting to follow the logic of the Somali, Oromo, Eritrean, and Tigrinean arguments for defining Ethiopia as colonialist and imperialist. A basic argument is that most of the Ethiopian periphery was conquered by force of arms during the late nineteenth century and that, in fact, colonial Ethiopia collaborated with the British, Italians, and French in partitioning the Horn of Africa. It is further argued that the Ethiopian conquest was brutal and cruel. In fact, documents uncovered by an Indian scholar confirm these allegations. British agents in the area reported to the Indian government in the late nineteenth century that the Ethiopian conquerors of the Ogaden "devastated" the country "massacring and driving out large numbers of the inhabitants." Other reports talked about "revolting cruelty"—about slaves tied to horses' tails and people being skinned alive.[23] Bereket Habte Selassie says that "where resistance was total the entire vanquished nation was sold into slavery."[24]

The secessionists emphasize that the Ethiopian state, whether under Haile Selassie or under Megistu Haile Mariam, is Amhara-dominated and that all the other peoples are in essence colonial subjects.[25] Cultural and linguistic oppression is cited as an important ingredient of Ethiopian colonialism. Teaching, preaching, broadcasting, or publishing in any language except Amharic was prohibited in the pre-1974 period. While this has changed, the separatists argue that forcible Amharization continues in all organs of state and in the educational system. Muslim Somalis, Afars, Eritreans, and Oromos also accused the Ethiopian state of religious persecution. Observers even dispute that there was a sincere effort on the part of the Amhara to truly assimilate subject nationalities by granting them equal rights and access to power. They argue that, as with the French and Portuguese in their colonies, the Amharas paid lip-service to true assimilation while essentially following a policy designed to maintain their supremacy.[26]

The policy to settle *naftaanya* (men with guns) in *katama* (military garrisons) in the territories conquered by Menelik is cited as further proof that the Amhara armed settlers were, for all intents and purposes, colonial settlers.[27] The policy of settling loyal Amhara among the subject nationalities is said to go back to Amda Tseyon's rule in the fourteenth century and continuing in Revolutionary Ethiopia (which established settler colonies after 1974 among the Anuak, Bertha, and Shanqella along the Sudanese border and in the Somali-Oromo areas of Harar, Bale, and Arusi). The Ethiopian settler system is said to be as economically exploitative as any other colonial settler system. Expropriation of land, forced labor, tax farming, and neglect of development in the peripheral areas are cited as examples of colonial exploitation. The Ethiopians vehemently refute the allegation that they were, or are, a colonial power. In addition to the salt water theory and the pigmentational-continental rationale (that only Europeans are colonialists), post-1974 Revolutionary Ethiopia also uses the intellectual arsenal of Marxism-Leninism in order to make the point that Ethiopia may have been feudal and oppressive but not colonial:

> In the Marxist-Leninist politico-economic sense, colonialism is and can only be a product of the premonopoly stages of capitalism. Such being the case, it is a self-evident truth that a colonial relationship does not possibly

exist between oppressor and oppressed nationalities in Ethiopia.... Ethiopia at present is not a multi-national colonial empire.[28]

Colonialization even in its primitive forms requires manufacture production. In its purer forms, it demands industrial production and capital.... Feudal Ethiopia did not possess any of the prerequisites ... with feudalism one can speak of conquest, not colonialization and this is quite a different matter.[29]

In order to prove their view that Ethiopia has never been colonial, the ruling Marxist-Leninists are ready to concede oppression, conquest, and feudalism, as historical "sins" that may be overcome. To concede colonialism would legitimize secession.

As in the Ethiopian case, the separatists in Southern Sudan claimed that their Arab opponents were colonialist and imperialist. They regarded themselves as a colony of the North. They employed the analogy with European colonialism in order to blur the distinction between anticolonial nationalism, which demanded secession from the empire in the name of self-determination, and postcolonial nationalism, which demanded secession from the independent postcolonial state:

To argue that the Sudan is to be recognized as one independent state is to slam the door on the sufferings ... of Angola and Mozambique which Portugal maintains are only "provinces" of the motherland. They are not the first in the history of mankind to have "their country" within the boundary of another. To recognize the Southern problem as a colonial case will therefore be a step in the right direction.[30]

Southerners regard Arab rule in the Sudan as colonial for almost the same reasons that Somalis and Eritreans regard Ethiopian rule as colonial. They talk about forcible occupation by the northern army which entered the South in 1955, the monopolization of all political power in Khartoum, the totally Arab character of the central bureaucracy, and the arrogance of Arab administrators in the South prior to 1972. Further evidence for the internal colonial regime is economic discrimination and exploitation and especially the Northern policy of "cultural expansionism and oppression."[31] Efforts to Arabize and Islamize the South by closing African-language schools, expelling Christian missionaries, imposing Islamic holidays in the 1950s and 1960s, declaring Sudan an Islamic state, applying Muslim law in the whole country, and reviving the Arabization of the Southern schools in the 1980s are, in the view of many Southerners, obvious colonial policies.

Many revisionists who fought the *status quo* defined their local African enemies as colonialist. Zanzibari Africans regarded Arab rule in the early 1960s as colonial. John Okello, who led the African revolt in Zanzibar, talked about "Arab colonialism."[32] The Saharwi still talk about Moroccon colonialism while in the 1960s and 1970s Muslim Chadians spoke about Christian Sara colonialism. Most Chadians condemned the Libyan intervention and partial occupation of Northern Chad as colonialist and imperialist as did many of black Africa's leaders (e.g., Omar Bongo, Siaka Stevens, Seyni Kountche, Sekou Touré, and Ahmadu Ahidjo).[33] Americo-Liberian rule in Liberia before 1980 has also been called "Black colonialism."[34] The definition of colonialism as a "political-economic relationship between a dominant Western nation and a subservient non-Western people" no longer enjoys general acceptance.[35] The revisionists and secessionists define colonialism as similar to Michael Hechter's "internal colonialism"—a term introduced to explain the English domination of its Celtic fringe (Scottish, Welsh, and Irish). Hechter's definition of the colonial periphery is based on economic exploitation and cultural discrimination:

> Commerce and trade among members of the periphery tend to be monopolised by members of the core. Credit is similarly monopolised. When commercial prospects emerge, bankers, managers, and entrepreneurs tend to be recruited from the core. The peripheral economy is forced into complementary development to the core, and thus becomes dependent on external markets. Generally, this economy rests on a single primary export, either agricultural or mineral. The movement of peripheral labour is determined largely by forces exogenous to the periphery. Typically there is great migration and mobility of peripheral workers in response to price fluctuations of exported primary products. Economic dependence is reinforced through juridical, political and military measures. There is a relative lack of services, lower standard of living and higher level of frustration, measured by such indicators as alcoholism, among members of the peripheral group. There is national discrimination on the basis of language, religion or other cultural forms. Thus the aggregate economic differences between core and periphery are causally linked to their cultural differences.[36]

Hechter's internal colony is different from an overseas colony by geographic contiguity and administrative integration and length of association with the center. George Balandier's "colonial situation" (domination by a racially and culturally different foreign conquering group, material inferiority, and an instrumental relationship between metropolis and colony) could, nevertheless, define internal colonies like Scotland, Catalonia, Kurdistan, the Amerindian areas in Latin America, or, in Africa, Southern Sudan, the Ogaden, the NFD, or Northern Chad (up to 1978).[37]

Black nationalists like Stokely Carmichael and Charles Hamilton have also talked about internal colonialism in the United States.[38] There is no doubt that the European-American notion of internal colonialism is a result of decolonization and the growing interest in colonial Africa. Curiously enough, the concept of internal colonialism developed in Europe and America was adopted by Eritreans, Somalis, Oromos, and Southern Sudanese in the 1970s and thus reimported to Africa.

In 1960, Plamenatz said that there is no basic difference between foreign rule within a state and a colonial government. He even thought that internal colonial subjects might be worse off because in a formal colony "dependence is not masked; it is public and open. There is not any hypocrisy about it."[39] In a formal colony, it is easy to mobilize international sympathy for the colonized, and separatist decolonization is viewed as legitimate and progressive. In an internal colony, on the other hand, nationalism may be used "as a cloak for oppression," separatism will be decried as reactionary and oppression of subject nationalities may be harsher than ever.[40] It is indeed a fact that many peoples in Africa were "reluctant decolonizers" because they feared repression and exploitation by the dominant ethnic groups. Among the reluctant decolonizers we may include the Hausa-Fulani in Nigeria, the Baganda in Uganda, the Africans in Zanzibar, the Lozi in Zambia, the Southern Sudanese, the Kenya Somalis, and the KADU tribes in Kenya. In 1959, the UN Visiting Mission to Rwanda encountered ruling Tutsi demonstrators with placards saying "Immediate Independence. Get rid of the Belgians for us." But the subject Hutus' mottoes were totally different: They shouted "Down with Tutsi feudalism. Long live Belgian trusteeship."[41] The concepts of internal colonialism may be of recent origin, but the fear expressed in the 1950s that "the remote and obvious foreigner actually in power may be felt to be less dangerous than the probable future ruler even though he is closer to the people" has come true for many Southern Sudanese, Kenya Somalis, Eritreans, or Saharwi.[42] When the Southern Sudanese Dunstan Wai wrote in 1983 that in the colonial period, it was "British colonial force which drove out the Northern aggressors and excluded them (as well as their language, religion, clothing and other cultural forms) and quite rightly so, from the South for 30 years," it is not difficult to guess that he preferred external to internal colonialism.[43]

The secessionists call for national self-determination *within* states. They attack Africa's boundaries as artificial and colonial and they argue that their peoples are subject to internal colonialism. In general, the fact that secessionists can effectively mobilize anticolonial slogans against the colonial partition and the colonial situation within the current states means that they can base their claims on a universally legitimized principle of national self-determination. This makes it easier for separatists to convince themselves and others that their cause is just. Mazrui demonstrated this point by letting an imaginary Baluba speak his mind:

> The so-called nationalists call me a tribalist and anti-African if I refuse to bow to some line drawn up by a conference in Berlin by white foreigners many, many years ago. They call me a stooge of the whites because I refuse to recognize a map drawn up by the whites or to accept concepts imported by the whites . . . As a Baluba tribesman, I am all for self-government—government of the Baluba, by the Baluba, for the Baluba.[44]

7

VIABILITY, BALKANIZATION, AND IRREVERSIBILITY

Every African nation has its Katanga.
Immanuel Wallerstein, 1961[1]

"If we were to redraw the map of Africa on the basis of religion, race or language, I fear many states will cease to exist."
Ethiopia's Prime Minister Aklilu Habta-Wäld, 1963[2]

In the question of independence and self-determination, viability is usually given a very, very low priority.
Biafra's leader Odemjegwu Ojukwu, 1968[3]

Are we to allow the principle of self-determination to be applied at the village level, at the district level, at the provincial level . . . Perhaps instead of having 146 states members of the United Nations we would have up to 1000.
Tanzania's UN representative Salim Ahmed Salim, 1973[4]

In freezing the status quo one generation which exercised its freedom of choice attempts to deprive later generations of the same freedom.
Harry Beran, 1984[5]

A major issue in the debate on national self-determination is the minimal or optimal size of the nation-state. Political philosophers since Plato have been divided over their preference for large or small states. Mazzini and Marx thought that only large nations should have the right to national self-determination.[6] For Mazzini, only a large nation could have a distinct mission, while for Marx, only a large nation based on a sizable market and rapid capital accumulation could create economic progress. Others presented opposite views. Kant and Rousseau, for instance, denied that liberty and equal

93

ity could be achieved in a large state.[7] They argued that only in a small community could decision making be democratic and the *volonté générale* ascertained. The basic disagreement between advocates of large and small states is reflected in attitudes towards the interpretation and implementation of national self-determination. The supporters of large states would be reluctant to legitimize small units to break up large states in the name of self-determination. Many opponents of the right of secession through self-determination argue that to confer the right of independent statehood to every people, however small, would create thousands of nonviable states. Basically, the opponents of small states argue that ministates lack the military power to defend themselves, have insufficient political standing to make their independence meaningful, and cannot use the economics of scale to achieve development and wealth. In their eyes, a host of ministates will perpetuate instability, dependence, and poverty. There are presently dozens of independent microstates (e.g., Barbados, Bermuda, Grenada, St. Lucia, St. Vincent, Bahrein, Maldive Islands, Qatar, Brunei, Kuwait, San Marino, Andorra, Lichtenstein, Monaco, Malta, and Luxemburg), and their proliferation is a nightmare for many supporters of big states.[8] They talk about the dangers of infinite divisibility and are haunted by "epidemic" separatism. Antony Smith confirms that "there is a demonstration effect of other successful ethnic nationalisms" and that the idea of national self-determination tends to be contagious.[9] The Pakistani UN delegate, who, in the Bangladesh debate of 1971, warned that "there will not be a Bangladesh only in Pakistan, there will be a Bangladesh everywhere" represents this epidemic point of view.[10] The opponents of secession approvingly quote Col. Edward House, Woodrow Wilson's adviser during the post-World War I peace conferences, who recalled that "no tribal entity was too small to have ambition for self-determination."[11] Woodrow Wilson himself conceded that "when I gave utterance to these words [that all nations had a right to self-determination], I said them without knowledge that nationalities existed which are coming to us every day."[12] Basically, the opponents of secession who want viable states say that once "things fall apart," and the "center cannot hold," "mere anarchy is loosed upon the world."[13]

There is, however, a different point of view which says that small, homogeneous states have done quite well in history. The "small is beautiful" school of thought would see in large states more alienation, bureaucratization, and repression, and in small states, more potential for genuine self-government, participation, and spontaneity. In their study on *Size and Democracy,* Dahl and Tufte came to the conclusion that there is no correlation between size, economic viability, and political survival.[14] To demonstrate how the viability argument may indeed be questionable, one could go back to Alfred Cobban's classical work, *The Nation-State and National Self-Determination,* published in 1944. In his book, Cobban presented the examples of Iceland and Malta to show the absurdity of national self-determination for nonviable entities. Today, both are legitimate members of the international community, as are dozens of other states of a similar size. Forbes represents an even more extreme point of view that even ministates like Monaco, San Marino, and Andorra do no harm to anyone. He regards the call for viable states as irrational and insincere and as based on the power interests of the larger powers and on their reluctance to grant their minorities the right of secession.[15] There is no doubt that nationalists frequently rationalized expansionism and planned to "swallow" small nations by resorting to the slogan of viability. In the nineteenth century, German nationalists like Fichte, List, and Treitschke thought a United Germany could only be viable if it included sizable territories of Germany's neighbors. Hitler's Germany rationalized expansionism as a quest for *Lebensraum* (living space), and so did Tojo's Japan.

The United Nations was ambivalent on the issue of state size. On the one hand, the UN, in principle, rejected secessions (e.g., Biafra, Katanga, Southern Sudan) and welcomed unions (e.g., Cameroun, Somalia, Tanzania, Equatorial Guinea), but on the other hand, it refused to limit self-determination to territories with a minimal size or a minimal population. Accordingly, the UN, in principle, favors national self-determination for the Pitcairn, Tokelau, and Nieu Islands who have a few thousand inhabitants, but rejects it for the Kurds or Southern Sudanese who number millions.

In Africa, the debate concerning the viability, stability, and potential balkanization of the existing states is similar to the nineteenth century debates in Europe. There is a widespread hostility against balkanization—the fragmentation of Africa into smaller and smaller units. In European history, the word "balkanization" refers to the processes of dissolution and disintegration in the Ottoman and Habsburg Empires during the nineteenth and twentieth centuries.[16] Nkrumah was so impressed by the significance of these developments—which began at the Congress of Vienna and culminated in the division of much of Europe into a host of small and weak nation-states—that he compared contemporary Africa with the Balkans, and this analogy was adopted by many other African leaders.[17] What is surprising is that African nationalists evidently overlooked the fact that European balkanization liberated many peoples from colonial or quasi-colonial rule. It is, consequently, difficult to understand the negative connotation which the concept has for a number of African politicians and scholars, because the breakup of these imperial systems was essentially a process of decolonization. The same arguments against the partition of Eastern Europe could have been, and, indeed, were, raised against the dissolution of the British and French Empires in Africa. According to Karl Deutsch, the driving force which broke up the Ottoman and Habsburg Empires was the nationalism of the Greeks, Serbs, Croats, Czechs, Bulgarians, Poles, and Rumanians.[18] Since it is difficult to understand how African anticolonial nationalists could be hostile to their European counterparts, it is fair to assume that their dislike of the concept of balkanization rests on a misreading of modern European history.

Widespread African opposition to ethnic revisionism is based on opposition to smallness, for many agree with Yakubu Gowon that ministates are a degradation of black people.[19] Obote vividly expressed this sentiment when he said "African nationalism hates small states."[20] Nkrumah identified balkanization with an Africa divided into "small, weak, and unstable states."[21] Much of the negative connotation attached to balkanized states has to do with their assumed small size.

The concept of balkanization is also frequently associated with strife. The numerous wars between the small nation-states which succeeded the Ottoman Empire brought about their identification with national jealousies and disputes. The fact that in other parts of that continent small countries coexisted in harmony and peace was simply disregarded. Nkrumah took over the European image of balkanization and its association with war: "It is now an indisputable historical fact that the creation of the small independent states in Europe provided the fertile soil out of which developed the national jealousies, dissensions and disputes which culminated in the First and Second World Wars."[22] It is questionable if any serious student of history can accept an analysis which overlooks many other factors, including the competitive ambitions of the big powers. To us, it is important that this image has been transferred to Africa. For Nkrumah, the military struggles in the Congo during the early 1960s represented the "Balkan Wars" of Africa.[23]

This hatred of small states and the belief in the intrinsic connection between size and viability leads to the rejection of secessionist self-determination. The Nigerian leadership, for example, rejected the viability of Biafra with its ten million people, oil resources, and high educational standards.[24] The secessions of Katanga, Southern Sudan, Eritrea, and Cabinda were similarly defined as unviable.

The concept of balkanization includes the idea of a chain reaction which, once started, is difficult to contain. Many view balkanization as a process of falling dominoes which is initiated the moment a precedent occurs and gains legitimacy. The speeches of Antony Enahoro during the Nigerian civil war best represent this alleged dynamic ingredient:

> Once fractionalization starts, it certainly will result in the further disintegration of the former Eastern Region of Nigeria. Neighbouring states with ethnic and other problems similar to ours will in due course also disintegrate, and a chain reaction will be set up all over Africa. Africa would end up in petty little principalities . . . once the right to secede was conceded, not only Nigeria but all the other multi-ethnic states of Africa would disintegrate.[25]

Others voiced similar sentiments. Jomo Kenyatta said that once secession is legitimized, "there would be no end to the exercise. Claims would heep upon claims and anarchy would be the result."[26] Other Kenyan leaders concurred with Kenyatta: Masinde Muliro raised the question, "what would remain of Kenya" if the Somalis unite with Somalia, the Luo and Abuluhya join their brothers in Uganda, and the coastal Nyika and inland Masai break away to be together with their people in Tanzania? Defense Minister Njoroge Mungai made the secessionist scenario even more ridiculous by saying that the Indian community in Pangani and the European settlers of Mathaiga may then want to secede and unite with India and the United Kingdom.[27] And Dahomey's Emile Zinsou warned that "if one admits the principle of secession, no one can say where it will end and a thousand reasons will be produced for areas to secede."[28]

Ethiopia, for example, which contains no less than eighty ethnic groups, was alarmed by the prospects of a secessionist "epidemy" should the Somalis and Eritreans succeed in their secession. The Ethiopian governments of Haile Selassie and Mengistu Haile Mariam both feared that the Somalis and Eritreans would be followed by the Oromos, Tigrineans, and Afars and that Ethiopia might then be reduced to a tiny, land-locked Amhara region. Because of the falling dominoes theory, opposition to secessionist self-determination is deeply implanted in Africa, and it matters little whether the fears of accelerated disintegration by precedents are rational or irrational.[29]

Another reason for the opposition to secessionist self-determination and balkanization is that balkanized states are generally depicted as the creation of the big powers.[30] Balkanization is regarded not only as the creation of colonialism or neocolonialism; it is also associated with dependence and weakness. In this context, the analogy with Europe is convincing and correct: the Balkan states have been described as "helpless pawns in the desperate game of the Great Powers."[31] In 1920, Lenin attacked "the deception which the imperialist powers systematically practice by creating in the guise of politically independent states, states which are absolutely dependent upon them economically, financially, and militarily."[32] Some forty years later, many African leaders agreed with this description of the effects of balkanization and emphasized the political and economic vulnerability of such states, a weakness which threatened to make their independence nominal.[33] For Nkrumah, balkanization in Europe arose "from the action of the great powers when they divided into a number of small and competing states the colonial possession of the Turkish Empire in Europe."[34] He believed that the "policy of creating several unstable and weak . . . states in Africa, was the same policy adopted by the great powers at the Congress of Vienna."[35] In other words, balkanized states are a product of colonialism, a primary tool of neocolonialism, and a result of alliances with imperialist forces. He believed that "the new Balkan states of Africa will not have the independence to shake off the economic shackles," and "so long as we remain balkanized . . . we shall be at the mercy of colonialism and imperialism."[36] While Nyerere accused the imperialists of perpetuating balkanization,[37] the All African People's Conference in Tunis in 1960 declared that balkanization was "a way to perpetuate neocolonialism."[38] Touré explained that balkanization must be feared as a "Machiavellian plan" by the big powers aimed "at dividing Africa in order to remain master of the continent."[39] The belief in, and the revolt against, foreign machinations and intrigues are part and parcel of all nationalisms. Nkrumah's and Touré's attacks on the balkanizing big powers are not essentially different from Fichte's tirade against those who meddled in German affairs in order to divide and rule Germany.[40] Another variant of the same theme is Buthelezi's condemnation of balkanization in South Africa as "a way to give white domination a breathing space."[41]

For some, balkanization is no threat, it is a reality. Pan-Africanists have always regarded the present states as nonviable, and because of that, call for pan-African unity.[42] Nyerere talked about the need for "removing" the balkanization of Africa.[43] In the early 1960s, he strongly supported the establishment of an East African Federation and, in 1964, Tanganyika and Zanzibar established the United Republic of Tanzania. Nkrumah always warned Africa not to remain balkanized.[44] The pan-Africanists would regard any further fragmentation as increasing the extent of existing balkanization. The same applies to the pan-Arabists. Qadhdhafi, for example, was never a strong supporter of POLISARIO's goal to establish a Saharan Republic because he basically supports a pan-Saharan or pan-Arab state and not nonviable and balkanized states.[45]

The viability argument also serves the opponents of secession in another way. They may argue that the whole is not viable if the part secedes. Zairian nationalists from Lumumba to Mobutu would say that Zaire is not viable without mineral-rich Katanga (Shaba). Mauritanian nationalists argue in the same way that separation of the black African populated Senegal River Valley, with its agricultural resources and skilled manpower, would make Mauritania an unviable strip of desert.[46] The same is true for oil-producing Cabinda and Angola, cotton-growing Sara Country and Chad, and oil-rich Biafra and Nigeria. In the case of Eritrea, the Ethiopians point out their dependence on the Eritrean ports of Massawa and Assab as Ethiopia's only outlets to the sea.

The revisionists try to refute the viability factor which helps to solidify the status quo. They point out that Africa's present sovereign nation-states were once labelled nonviable and balkanized. The colonialists, while opposing demands for independence, ridiculed the viability of the colonies. In 1948, Haile Selassie claimed Somalia for Ethiopia because "we do not believe such a state can be viable standing alone separated from Ethiopia."[47] In

1966, he said the same about Djibouti. Today, both Somalia and Djibouti are independent states. In the 1940s, Egyptian nationalists said an independent Sudan was unviable, and in the 1950s and 1960s, the Moroccans said the same about Mauritania.

In French West Africa, the federalists, led by Senghor, opposed the breakup of the AOF by the *Loi-Cadre* of 1956. They regarded a separate statehood for Senegal, Guinea, Upper Volta, Ivory Coast, Soudan (Mali), Dahomey (Benin), Mauritania, and Niger as balkanization into nonviable states. In 1958, Senghor declared Guinea's "non" in de Gaulle's plébiscite to be an act of balkanization because it undid his hopes for the reconstitution of the AOF at a later stage.[48] Today, all the eight AOF territories are independent states that have been viable for almost three decades. The leaders of French Equatorial Africa—Youlou, Dacko, M'ba, and Tombalbaye—declared as late as February 1960 that the AEF would have to become one internationally sovereign state with internal autonomy for its constituent parts. They declared a separate independence for Congo-Brazzaville, Chad, Gabon, and the Central African Republic to be "ridiculous" because these territories were too small and too poor for statehood.[49] A few months later all four became independent states.

The All African Peoples Conference, which convened in Tunis in 1960, supported the creation of a Greater Morocco and described the independence of Mauritania as balkanization. The AAPC also demanded that Katanga and Buganda remain within Zaire and Uganda respectively, that Zambia be a part of an independent Central Africa, and that Togo join Ghana.[50] Two of these four political entities are now independent states. Today, nobody makes the distinction between balkanized Mauritania, Zambia, or Togo, and nonbalkanized Ghana or Morocco.

For the school of thought which defines the status quo as balkanized and which opposed the creation of several new states in 1960, the existing system has simply become more balkanized. For those who regard only secession as balkanization, and who opposed the breakup of the AOF or the independence of Mauritania, Togo, or Zambia, the results have, interestingly enough, ceased to be controversial—although future secessions would again be viewed in a derogatory fashion. This intellectual inconsistency reflects the confusion over what degree of fragmentation constitutes balkanization.

Revisionists do emphasize the existence of a host of small states in Africa. They insist that it is difficult to dispute the viability of Biafra, Katanga, Eritrea, and Southern Sudan and to accept the viability of the Cape Verde Islands, the Comoros, Sao Tome and Principe, the Seychelles, Djibouti, Equatorial Guinea, Gambia, Mauritius, Lesotho, and Swaziland. Even fairly large states like Mauritania, Chad, Botswana, and the not yet independent Namibia have small populations compared to Biafra or the Southern Sudan

(Biafra's population was even larger than that of Tanzania, Kenya, Uganda, Zambia, Malawi, and other fairly large African states). The comparison with other states led Dahomey's President Emile Zinsou to ask the rhetorical question why eight million Ibos should not be granted the right of self-determination and become a nation.[51]

Secessionists, as a rule, reject the nonviability of their homelands and peoples. Biafra's Ojukwu brushed aside any notion that Biafra should be opposed because of nonviability by declaring that considerations of viability play no role in struggles for independence. Historically, Ojukwu is on solid ground. Recent history, both in Europe and the Third World, has shown that for determined small nations, which aim to secede from a larger empire or state and achieve national liberation, the concept of viability is quite irrelevant. Most struggles for independence and self-determination have been fought in opposition to the viability argument of the status quo power. Colonialism, itself, argued that the mother country could not be viable without its colonies and the colonies could not be viable without the mother country. Anticolonialism had to overcome the viability argument by posing liberation as an antithesis. The Eritreans counter any notions that Eritrea might be nonviable by emphasizing Eritrea's industrial base, its network of paved roads, its mineral deposits (gold, copper, zinc, nickel, and manganese), and its ports and skilled manpower. Northern Nigeria's Ahmadu Bello, who wanted a Northern secession in the early 1950s, declared that the North is "certainly viable."[52] Similar sentiments were voiced by the leaders of CONAKAT (in Katanga), FLEC (in Cabinda), and the Anyanya (in Southern Sudan).

During the Biafran crisis, Nyerere even argued that "when a large number of people stop believing that the state is theirs then it is no longer viable."[53] According to Nyerere, a "whole" is not "viable" if it does not treat its "parts" fairly.

The revisionists also reject the domino theory implied in the concept of balkanization. The perception of balkanization as a continuing dynamic process prevented many potential supporters of Biafra from granting recognition to the secessionists. Ojukwu explained that "a country never disintegrates because another one did, otherwise there would be only fragments of countries left in the world today—after all there have been many precedents for disintegration."[54] On the other hand, he remained a prisoner of the chain reaction theory, seeking to assure other African leaders that the secession of Biafra would not become a precedent—indeed, that it would be a warning:

> We Biafrans are satisfied that Biafra may yet prove to be a lesson for the furtherance of unity in other states of Africa . . . rather than a precedent for disintegration . . . Never again in Africa will one nation of a political community seek with impunity the total annihilation of another community.[55]

What we have demonstrated very clearly to Africa is how not to treat minorities. I do not think anybody would want to face this problem again.[56]

Nyerere argued that the domino theory had been used by imperialists and that Churchill had used the same rationalization to defend his opposition to India's independence. Nevertheless, Tanzanian newspapers conceded that the fear of progressive disintegration and balkanization was legitimate and real and called for a recognition of Biafra for humanitarian reasons, rather than because of a general rejection of the domino theory.

Ojukwu has been a lonely voice in the attempt to refute the anarchic picture attributed to balkanization:

For a time there were endless wars in Europe; incessant conflicts until the old European empires were dismantled, until the Balkans were balkanized—then came peace.[57]

Europe found peace through balkanization, why not Africa through Biafranization. By balkanization Europe gave proof to the truth that all conflict has its root cause in the desire of one party to dominate the other. We propose the same answer—sovereignty for nations that assert their right for self-determination.[58]

The African scholar Kamanu also refutes the domino theory that says that one secession will necessarily lead to an endless chain of secessions. He argues that the dissolution of the African giants (Nigeria, Zaire) would enhance the prospects of African unity by making for more equality and less fear about hegemony among the African states. Kamanu thinks a rigid adherence to the "sanctity of borders formula" solidifies the present state system and makes greater unity more difficult.[59] Kamanu also empirically disputes the domino theory of secession by citing the examples of successful post-World War II secessions in Asia: Syria, Singapore, and Bangladesh. One could add European secessions like Norway (1905), Ireland (1921), and Iceland (1944). In none of these cases was secession a precedent for additional secessions; there was no chain reaction of falling dominoes.

Nevertheless, even the minimalists accept the need for a required minimum size of territory and population. They also have to face the question of how small is small and how small is too small? Otherwise, one may reach the *absurdum* of self-determination for two individuals. To demand a minimal viability is quite logical; the problem is that it is a sheer impossibility to reach consensus on the viable minimum. Nyerere, who supported the Biafran secession, emphasized that the right of national self-determination applies only to *large* ethnic groups. Kamanu agrees that "like individual freedom, collective freedom has its limits. The right to self-determination cannot mean the freedom of every self-distinguishing ethnocultural group to secede."[60] That means that even the most generous interpretation of the principle of national self-determination leaves out small peoples. The UN Charter promises national self-determination for *all* peoples, but *all* peoples will never have the right to self-determination.

In general, all secessionists argue that theirs is a special case and that no dominoes will fall. The way the Somalis reconcile the support for secessionism in Ethiopia and Kenya with their opposition to balkanization and falling dominoes is only one example. The Somali leaders regard the status quo as responsible for the fragmentation of their nation. They do not see any intrinsic contradiction between their opposition to balkanization and their aspiration to a Greater Somalia which entails the support of secession in eastern Kenya and southern Ethiopia:

> The principle of self-determination when used properly to unify and enlarge an existing state with a view towards its absorption in a federal system of government is neither balkanization nor fragmentation. It is a major contribution to unity and stability . . . We refuse to be "balkanized" . . . We are . . . a single Somali nation.[61]

Another question inherent in the concept of national self-determination is whether self-determination, once decided upon, is a "one shot affair"[62] or a "plébiscite de tous les jours."[63] Is the decision of a people to belong to this or that nation and nation-state reversible or irreversible? A recognized right to reversibility may bring about constant changes in the international state-system, an unending chain of border adjustments, and may prevent the consolidation of a stable world order. The right of reversibility will also immediately raise the question of how often the population of a territory will have the opportunity to reverse its decision: once in a century, every decade, every year, every day? If reversibility is denied for the sake of order and stability, self-determination for one generation may very well mean the denial of self-determination for future generations. If a people's decision is irreversible, does that people not become a prisoner within legitimate, self-determined boundaries with no way to escape once the conditions have changed? Kedourie cannot resist asking if the right of national self-determination without the right of reversibility is not, from the point of view of future generations, as arbitrary as conquests and secret diplomacy.[64] In fact, it is not easy to argue that in an age where "divorce is permitted, employment relationships can be terminated and governments can be voted out of office" that peoples should not have the right from time to time to reconsider under what sovereignty they want to live.[65]

In general, the status quo powers insist on irreversibility of self-determination, while the revisionists demand reversibility. From 1792 to 1793, France annexed Nice, Savoy, Avignon, and Vennaissin after plebiscites were held in these areas. Once they became a part of France, it was deemed a crime punishable by death to call for a reversal of that decision by a new plebiscite. In the American Civil War, the North opposed the secession of the South because it regarded the decision by the states to form a federal union as irreversible. In 1871, German nationalists denied the population of Alsace-Lorraine the right to self-determination because what mattered for them was that, in the past, the population had made an irreversible decision to attach the area to the German Empire. Whether this historical decision is true or fictitious is debatable, but what is clear is that, for the German nationalists, the wishes of the people in 1871 were irrelevant.[66]

In Africa, the same logic of irreversibility applies. In the final days of decolonization, there was some room for reversibility. In 1958, most French colonies decided in a plebiscite to stay with France, but in 1960, they decided to reverse their decision. In 1966, Djibouti voted to stay French, and a decade later it, too, decided to become independent. After the African states had gained independence, they invoked irreversibility against the dangers of secession and balkanization. The Nigerian leaders argued that Biafra (as Eastern Nigeria) exercised its right to self-determination by making an irreversible decision in 1960 to be part of an independent Nigerian Federation. The Ethiopians argued the same with regard to Eritrea's irreversible decision to join Ethiopia in 1952. In fact, most Ibos strongly supported the independence of the Nigerian Federation in 1960, but by 1967, almost all Ibos had reversed their decision and wholeheartedly supported secessionist Biafra. In Eritrea, we have a similar situation: the Christian Tigrineans who supported the union with Ethiopia in the late 1940s and early 1950s became completely disillusioned with Ethiopian rule in the 1960s and have, since then, supported the Eritrean secessionists in ever increasing numbers. In both cases, the concept of irreversibility was upheld, although the people involved wanted to reverse their earlier support for the central government. It is doubtful whether it can be said in good faith that the Southern Sudanese agreed in 1956 to be part of the Sudan. According to Dunstan Wai, herein lies the major difference between the Biafran and Southern Sudanese case:

Whereas the Biafrans were at the vanguard of Nigeria's decolonization politics and participated fully in the negotiations which led to the independence of Nigeria, and were, indeed, partners with Northern Nigerians in the first Federal Republic, the Southern Sudanese were not involved in the independence movement, did not want a union of the North and South, and were denied participation in the discussions which gave final shape to the constitutional framework prior to independence. The Biafrans entered into a political contract with the rest of Nigerians on the eve of independence, but the Southern and Northern Sudanese did not. That explains why the Southern Sudanese launched their war of independence before complete British imperial withdrawal from the Sudan.[67]

Some Southern Sudanese even go beyond the denial that the South agreed to be part of a united Sudan and specifically speak about the right to reversible self-determination: "The Front (the Southern Sudanese 'Southern Front') contended that even if people of the South had agreed to be part of the North which they did not, self-determination by a people could be exercised more than once."[68]

The Arab North, nevertheless, vehemently stressed its point of view that the South acceded to independence in 1956 as part of a united Sudan and by that made an irreversible decision not to go on its own and establish Southern Sudanese independence. The doctrine of irreversibility, which aims to consolidate the current state system, discourage secession, and sanctify the borders, cannot prevent bloody confrontations between the adherents of the status quo and the revisionists for the simple reason that national sentiments, loyalties, and identities are in constant flux. They have never been permanent and static, and it is hard to believe that Africa will prove to be the exception to this general rule.

8

CONFLICTING PRINCIPLES

No people must be forced under a sovereignty under which it does not wish to live.

Woodrow Wilson, 1917[1]

All peoples have the right to self-determination; by virtue of that right they freely determine their political status and freely pursue their economic, social and cultural development.

UN Declaration on the Granting of Independence to Colonial Countries and Peoples, 1960[2]

The Member States—solemnly affirm and declare their adherence to the following principles:

1. the sovereign equality of all member states
2. non-interference in the internal affairs of states
3. respect for the sovereignty and territorial integrity of each state and for its inalienable right to independent existence
4. peaceful settlement of disputes by negotiation, mediation, conciliation and arbitration.

OAU Charter, Article III, 1963[3]

We have analyzed conflicting interpretations of the principle of national self-determination and the dilemmas inherent in the concept itself. In addition, we must also examine the relationship between the principle of national self-determination and other basic norms and values of international politics. Even the staunchest supporters of the right of peoples to self-determination do not claim that the right of self-determination is necessarily superior to other rights and principles in *all* instances. The 1950 UN resolution on Eritrea, which decided to make Eritrea an "autonomous unit to be federated with Ethiopia under the sovereignty of the Ethiopian Crown," offers a good example for the potential conflict between the principle of national self-determination and other principles or rights. The resolution pretends to take into consideration "the wishes and welfare of the inhabitants of Eritrea," "the interests of peace and security in East Africa," the "rights and claims of Ethiopia based on geographical, historical, ethnic or economic reasons," and "Ethiopia's legitimate need for adequate access to sea."[4] The crucial question is certainly whether all these principles are complementary and, if not, which are the principles that have to prevail, and which are the principles that are to be sacrificed.

Both the UN and OAU Charters contain an inherent contradiction between the principle of national self-determination and the right of states to preserve and defend their territorial integrity. The UN Charter calls for the "right of self-determination of *peoples*" and states its opposition to "any attempt aimed at the partial or total disruption of the national unity and the territorial integrity of a *country*."[5] (Italics added.) The OAU Charter insists both on the "inalienable right of all *peoples* to control their own destiny" and on "respect for the sovereignty and territorial integrity of each *state*."[6] (Italics added.) In both cases, the principles of self-determination and territorial integrity are complimentary only if there is a complete overlap between "peoples," "countries," and "states." The conflict between the right of states to territorial integrity and the right of nations (or peoples) to self-determination has its roots in the beginnings of modern nationalism in the late eighteenth century. Two hundred years after the French Revolution, this basic contradiction between states and peoples remains a fundamental problem of the international community, whether we speak of the Arab World, the Soviet Union, India, China, Spain, Yugoslavia, Canada, or Great Britain.

In Africa, more than anywhere else, we face the dilemma of having to choose between territorial integrity of a state and the self-determination of a people. The conflict between these two principles explains most of the wars, conflicts, and tensions between and within African states in postcolonial Africa. There were secessionist or irredentist conflicts in Nigeria, Zaire, Ethiopia, Sudan, Uganda, Kenya, and the Western Sahara and, to a lesser extent, in Chad, Mali, Zambia, Angola, Mauritania, Equatorial Guinea, the Ivory Coast, and the Comoros. King Hassan II of Morocco, for example, insists on the territorial integrity of the Moroccan state, including the newly liberated and reunified Western Sahara, while his opponents in the Western Sahara demand self-determination for the Saharwi people. Haile Selassie, in his opening speech at the founding conference of the OAU in May 1963, reiterated that Ethiopia's foreign policy is based on "noninterference in the internal affairs of states, respect for the territorial integrity and sovereignty of nations and the peaceful settlement of disputes."[7] He was careful not to include the principle of national self-determination, and it is likely that his set of principles was designed to forestall any Somali claims to national self-determination. On the other hand, during the Biafra-Nigeria war Nyerere showed that even an African with the best nationalist credentials will not always accept the superiority of territorial integrity over self-determination: "It is foolish for Africans to stand by idly while millions of Africans are being killed by other Africans in the name of territorial integrity."[8] The Somalis also, for obvious reasons, have strongly opposed the territorial integrity of states as a legitimate core value. They argue that states are means to an end— the welfare, liberty, and self-determination of a nation. They argue that sanctity, integrity, or inviolability should not be attributed to the state, and that the means should not become the end. They say that the state has to serve the people and not vice versa. The problem is that people in power don't always think that way.

Sometimes, the very existence of the state—not only its territorial integrity—is invoked as a value higher than national self-determination. In the midnineteenth century, the Hungarian nationalist leader Kossuth told a Rumanian delegation, which came to plead for national self-determination for the Rumanians in Hungary, that their demands were unacceptable: "Shall Hungary then not be a state? Shall each of the races inhabiting it demand a separate state on its own account? With such principles either Hungary will break up or the sword will decide."[9] How similar do African leaders sound when they declare separatism to be a mortal danger not only to the integrity but also to the very survival of states? Madagascar's and Mali's former presidents Philibert Tsiranana and Modibo Keita said it bluntly:

> Should we take race, religion or language as criteria for setting up boundaries a few states in Africa will be blotted out from our map.[10]

> . . . if we desire that our nations should be ethnic entities speaking the same language and having the same psychology, then we shall find no single veritable nation in Africa.[11]

Another international principle which may conflict with the right of peoples to national self-determination is the principle of noninterference in the internal affairs of states. The norm of noninterference clearly conflicts with external support for secessionist self-determination. Supporters of the principle of national self-determination and the right of secession argue that every people has to gain its own liberation without outside interference. No people, however, can achieve secessionist self-determination without a certain amount of outside support ranging from full military intervention (as in the case of India's invasion of Bangladesh) to international diplomatic recognition (as in the case of Syria which seceded from the Egyptian-led United Arab Republic and achieved instant recognition by the big powers). Without some outside intervention, the peoples of the Habsburg and Ottoman Empires would not have gained their freedom. The oppressed peoples under Nazi rule would not have been liberated, and the process of decolonization would never have succeeded. The denial of outside support for secessionists fighting for self-determination constitutes support for the central government in its suppression of secessionist movements. This kind of noninterference is thus diametrically opposed to the principle of self-determination, at least in the eyes of the peoples fighting for secessionist self-determination. In Africa, the Biafrans, Southern Sudanese, Katangese, Eritreans, and Somalis could rightly point out that the principled opposition to separatism by the UN, OAU, and most African governments constitutes interference in the internal affairs of sovereign states. If intervention is defined as "any activity across geographical boundaries organized or unorganized to shore up a threatened authority structure or to facilitate the emergence of a new one out of a larger country," any principled opposition to separatism certainly constitutes interference in the internal affairs of states.[12] Noninterference would have demanded a refusal to take sides in the *internal* wars between Biafrans and Nigerians, Southern Sudanese and Arabs, Eritreans and Ethiopians. By declaring its opposition to separatism, the African establishment has definitely taken sides.

The principle of noninterference in the internal affairs of states has always been of doubtful morality. Noninterference may have meant continued oppression whether in Hitler's Germany, Pol Pot's Cambodia, Amin's Uganda, Micombero's Burundi, or Apartheid South Africa. In the nineteenth century, it was regarded as perfectly legitimate for Palmerston's and Gladstone's England to assist peoples in the Balkans who rose up in arms against Ottoman oppression. Noninterference may not only conflict with national self-determination, but may actually mean the abandonment of peoples to an oppressive fate. Walzer has the moral sensitivity to justify intervention in cases of "enslavement and massacre."[13] Secessionists fighting for independence can often rightly claim to have suffered enslavement and massacre.

Sometimes, the principle of national self-determination is pushed aside because it conflicts with the security of a particular state or with the requirements of international peace and stability. After World War I, self-determination was not granted to the Southern Tyrolese, Sudeten Germans, and the people of Alsace-Lorraine because the territories involved were regarded as vital to the security of Italy, Czechoslovakia, and France. In general, the right of nations to self-determination is very often diametrically opposed to the internationally recognized right of states to self-defense. Austria was denied the right to join Germany because a "Greater Germany" was perceived as a threat to international peace and security. For the sake of regional peace between Turkey and Greece, Cyprus was denied the right to choose unification with Greece in 1960. Events in Central Europe in the 1930s illustrate the fact that national self-determination may indeed be exploited to undermine international peace and security. In the name of national self-determination, Hitler ordered his troops into the Rhineland, Austria, Czechoslovakia, and Poland. Lloyd George said it bluntly: "We should not push the principle of self-determination so far as unduly to strengthen any state which is likely to be a cause of danger to European peace."[14]

In Africa, one could very well argue that the antisecessionist domino theory is based on the assumption that further balkanization of Africa has to be avoided for the sake of continental stability, peace, and security. While Herder, John Stuart Mill, Mazzini, and Woodrow Wilson believed in peace *by* national self-determination, the domino theory of the OAU is better defined as peace *or* national self-determination. When it perceives ethnocultural self-determination as conflicting with a peaceful and stable world order, the OAU follows the UN. As *organizations,* both are committed to oppose the right of secession. Djibouti is analogous to Cyprus: its right to unification with Somalia was forfeited because a vote for Greater Somalia would certainly have brought about an all-out war between Ethiopia and Somalia.

In many of Africa's postcolonial wars, the right of secessionist self-determination was opposed by the right of states to defend themselves. When the Somalis invaded Ethiopia in 1977, their aim was the national liberation of the Somali *people* in the Ogaden, but from the Ethiopian point of view, what was involved was the right of the Ethiopian *state* to defend itself. The Southern Sudanese fought for national self-determination of the Southern Sudanese, but the Northern Sudanese fought back to defend the Sudan as a state against a secession supported by some of Sudan's neighboring states. The Saharwi are fighting for national self-determination. The Moroccans, on the other hand, not only believe in historical Morocco but also regard an independent Western Sahara allied to Algeria as encirclement and a danger to Moroccan state security. The spectre of encirclement by hostile Muslim states has also loomed large in Ethiopia's opposition to the separatist aspirations of the Eritreans, Somalis, Afars, and Oromos. Not only military security but also mixed strategic-economic considerations may conflict with the principle of national self-determination. Danzig became an internationalized free city not because the population so desired, but because of the overriding concern to secure for Poland an outlet to the sea. Eritrea bears a certain analogy to Danzig because Ethiopia's right to gain a strategic and economically vital outlet to the sea was one reason why the UN decided against Eritrean independence and why all Ethiopian governments have so insistently rejected Eritrean demands for national self-determination and the right of secession.

Other principles which may collide with the right to national self-determination are nonuse of force and the principle that international agreements have to be observed (*pacta sunt servanda*). In almost all separatist cases, the people fighting for self-determination can expect success only by resorting to violence against the military, the police, the courts, and bureaucracy of the central government. Kedourie's argument that any attempt to change the political map of Africa according to the principle of national self-determination of ethnocultural selves may be a "brutal and sanguinary affair" is certainly accurate.[15] Sometimes, the wish to homogenize the population of a territory and to conform *pro forma* to the principle of self-determination may lead to expulsions of peoples from territories with mixed populations, thus changing the boundaries of peoples instead of the boundaries of states. Robert Lansing was right that the principle of national self-determination has caused "enough despair, enough suffering and enough anarchy."[16] The question remains whether without the principle there would not have been even more violence and oppression. Separatists are rebels against the legally recognized status quo. They are revisionists in the sense that they want to revise the legal order, including laws, constitutions, and international conventions. Their revisionism has to run counter to the *pacta sunt servanda* principle of international law. For example, one of the first acts of independent Somalia, in 1960, was to abrogate all international treaties which accorded international legal legitimacy to the boundaries which divided the Somali people.

Above all, the principle of national self-determination often entails a denial of the same right to a competing self. Claims for national self-determination most frequently conflict with claims of other selves for national self-determination, rather than with qualitatively wholly different claims.

9

THE PROBLEM OF THE
DOUBLE STANDARD

You know as well as we do that right, as the world goes, is an issue only between equals in power and that the strong do what they can and the weak submit.

The Athenians to the Melians, Thucydides[1]

All nice people like Us are We and everybody else is They.

Rudyard Kipling[2]

Secession could be tolerated as long as one favored the secessionist.

P.H. Judd, 1965[3]

How many years can some people exist
Before they are allowed to be free
The answer my friend is blowing in the wind
The answer is blowing in the wind.

J.N. Saxena, 1978[4]

"Using a double standard means applying different criteria to situations which are so similar that they merit equal treatment."[5] Lloyd George once observed in despair how "small nations who have hardly leapt into the light of freedom begin immediately to oppress their minorities."[6] Emerson, too, became quite cynical about the use and misuse of the principle of national self-determination: "My right to self-determination against those who oppress me is obviously unimpeachable, but your claim to exercise such a right against me is wholly inadmissable."[7] There is no doubt that the right of national self-determination is indeed a "chameleonic right."[8]

Revolutionary France granted the right of self-determination to those who wanted to join "*la patrie*" and denied it to those who wished to secede.

Napoleon conquered Europe in the name of self-determination, but ruthlessly suppressed those who took up arms against the French occupation, whether in Prussia or Haiti. Barère proclaimed "liberty and equality— these are our rights, unity and indivisibility—these our maxims."[9] Wherever it was opportune, liberty was granted; otherwise, indivisibility was proclaimed.

Mazzini demanded ethnocultural self-determination for Italy and all of Europe, but in order to transcend the linguistic boundary and to claim German-speaking South Tyrol for Italy he invoked Roman history and declared that the landscape speaks Italian.[10] When a Slovak delegation approached the Hungarian freedom fighter Kossuth to ask for autonomy for Slovakia, Kossuth told them that his map did not show any Slovakia.[11] The liberal German nationalists who gathered in the *Paulskirche* in 1848 proclaimed German unity and democracy, but refused to grant Danes, Poles, Czechs, and Slovenes the right of secession.

Marx supported self-determination for the Irish in order to weaken the British ruling class and for the Poles in order to weaken Czarist Russia. He opposed national self-determination for Serbs, Croats, Slovaks, Czechs, and other small "reactionary" Slavic peoples because the political independence of the Southern Slavs would have strengthened Russia, the prime enemy of the revolution.[12] Lenin proclaimed the right of peoples to self-determination and secession, but left the possibility open to deny this very right because "the proletariat . . . evaluates every national demand, every national separation from the angle of the class struggle of the workers."[13] On another occasion, Lenin explained that "our unqualified recognition of the struggle for the right of self-determination does not commit us to support every demand for national self-determination."[14] In the policy of the Soviet Union, this ideological flexibility provided the legitimacy for opportunism. In principle, the Soviets recognize the right of secession, but they put an end to the independence of Armenia, Georgia, the Ukraine, Buchara, Azerbaidshan, and the Baltic States by force of arms. The Soviet Union supported the unity of all Ukrainians and Byelorussians, but always by annexing territories to the Soviet Union, never by allowing secession from the Soviet Union. They were strong supporters of anticolonial self-determination, as long as it was far away from home. They insisted on true national self-determination for the five thousand inhabitants of Nauru, but agreed only to fictitious independence for the fifty million Ukrainians.

The Chinese and Vietnamese communists are no better. For thirty years, Mao Tse Tung promised the Tibetans, Mongols, Uighurs, and Chuang the right of self-determination and the right of secession. When he seized power in 1949, he proclaimed the minority areas "inalienable parts" of China.[15] The fighting Viet Minh made the same promises to the Muong, Meo, and Khmer, but independent Vietnam, according to its constitution, is "one and indivisible," and in 1975, even the regional autonomy of the minorities was abolished.[16]

The American Declaration of Independence is based on the right of self-determination and secession from the orbit of the British Empire. Later on, the United States fought the Southern secession in the name of "unity" and "indivisibility." After the Civil War, the United States became an opponent of secession (e.g., in the cases of Biafra, Eritrea, Southern Sudan, the Ogaden, or Bangladesh), but when it suited its regional or global interests, as in Panama in 1903, in Tibet in the 1950s, and in Iraqi Kurdistan in the 1960s, the United States encouraged separatism.

In 1917, Woodrow Wilson became the champion of national self-determination for subject peoples and proclaimed the principle to be the cornerstone of a just world order. The British Prime Ministers Asquith and Lloyd George proclaimed that Britain was fighting the war for "the rights of smaller nationalities."[17] At the same time, they signed secret treaties with Russia and Italy in which they committed themselves to the transfer of Austrian, Greek, Albanian, Croatian, and Turkish territories to Italian and Russian rule. In Ireland, Egypt, and India, people who fought for national self-determination were imprisoned and executed. In the post-World War I peace settlement, the principle of self-determination was only applied where it weakened the enemy states (Germany, Austria, Hungary, Turkey), but was disregarded where it would not have been favorable to the Allies (e.g., in the cases of Southern Tyrol, the Sudeten, Danzig, Alsace-Lorraine). Cobban cynically called what happened at the peace conferences "national determinism" instead of "national self-determination." Wherever the Allies would have lost a plebiscite, there was no plebiscite. In Eastern Europe, the Czechs, Serbs, and Poles succeeded in establishing themselves as independent and dominant nations in newly independent states, but they refused to grant the right of self-determination to the Croats, Slovenes, Slovaks, and the Ukrainians.

During World War II, Churchill and Roosevelt issued a call for self-determination in the Atlantic Charter, but Churchill refused to apply it to India and the colonies of the British Empire. In the Indian subcontinent, India denied self-determination to Kashmir, but fought for the self-determination of Bangladesh, while Pakistan insisted on self-determination for Kashmir and denied it to Bangladesh. Indonesia, which fought for the incorporation of West-Irian in the 1960s and proclaimed that national self-determination is applicable only within colonial boundaries, went beyond these boundaries in 1975 and swallowed the former Portuguese Timor by armed force.

In Africa, there is no less inconsistency and opportunism in applying the principle of national self-determination. Many see anticolonial self-determination as a supreme good, while they regard ethnic self-determination as the height of evil. Even this principle is frequently broken and the double standard reigns supreme.

The Muslim-Arab states of Africa clearly seem to differentiate between *"Dar al Islam"* (the domain of Islam) and *"Dar al Harb"* (the domain of war).[18] All the North African states (with the exception of Tunisia) strongly supported Nigeria in its war against Biafra. The completely Christian character of Biafra, the Ibos' self-perception as the "Jews of Africa," and the central role of the Muslim North in the Gowon coalition explain the strong Arab engagement against Biafra.[19] The same applies also to the Southern Sudan— no Arab state supported its secession from Arab Sudan between 1955 and 1972. On the other hand, Muslim Eritrean separation from Christian Ethiopia had strong support in the Arab and Muslim World. Nasser, who sent bombers and pilots to Nigeria to fight Biafran secessionism, supported Eritrean secessionism with money, broadcasting services, and office space in Cairo. Algeria's president, Houari Boumedienne, delivered a firey speech against Biafran separatism in the Algiers OAU summit in 1968 and, on the very same day, allowed the ELF to open offices in the Algerian capital.[20] In the early 1960s, the irredentist demands of Morocco with regard to Mauritania were supported by Egypt, Libya, Sudan, Algeria, Black Muslim Mali, and Guinea. None of these states supported any Christian revisionism, whether in Katanga, Biafra, or the Southern Sudan. The Muslim-Arab states were generally also strong supporters of pan-Somalism. All Islamic conferences passed resolutions in support of Somali and Eritrean separatism and insisted on the right of all Muslim peoples "to determine their own future."[21] The Arab League passed similar resolutions, although they contradicted OAU principles. The double standard is especially striking in the cases of Sudan and Somalia. Sudan fought a bitter war to suppress separatism in the South. At the same time, it supported Eritrean and Somali separatism in Ethiopia. Certainly, it was a matter of "I help your rebels because you help mine," but even in times of peace in the Southern Sudan (e.g., 1976–1977) Numeiri declared his support for Eritrean independence.[22] Somalia was no different. While mobilizing the Muslim world for its irredentism, it declared its total opposition to Biafran separatism and its support for the "unity and national integrity of Nigeria."[23] The religiously tinged double standard was even more widespread. The radical, but Muslim, Sekou Touré was all in favor of a Greater Morocco and a Greater Somalia, but staunchly opposed Biafran revisionism. More intriguing were the attitudes of the main antagonists in the Nigerian-Biafran War towards Ethiopia and Eritrea. In order not to antagonize the Muslim-Arab bloc, Gowon refrained from taking sides against the Muslim Eritrean and Somali separatists in Ethiopia, while Ojukwu courted the Christian antiseparatist government of Emperor Haile Selassie. In general, there was much sympathy for Biafra in Christian Africa, which at least partially identified the struggle as a Muslim-Christian confrontation. This goes a long way to explain why even countries which faced separatist problems either supported Biafra (Zambia, Ivory Coast) or tended towards neutrality (Uganda, Ethiopia).

Ethiopia insists on the sanctity of the colonial boundaries in the Ogaden and denies the legitimacy of the colonial boundaries in Eritrea. It is fiercely opposed to separatism at home, but not so fiercely in Northern Somalia and Southern Sudan. Since it adopted Marxism-Leninism in the mid 1970s, it has also adopted the Marxist-Leninist double standard with regard to national self-determination and the right of secession. On the one hand, Ethiopia supports "progressive" self-determination, "progressive" rights of nations, and "progressive" secession. On the other hand, opposition to national self-determination is also legitimate if self-determination is declared "reactionary" and inhibiting to the proletarian revolution.[24] The rule is that secession is to be supported or condemned according to whether "the demand promotes or retards, strengthens or weakens, advances or modernizes the revolutionary class struggle of the proletariat."[25] This sophisticated dialectic enabled the Dergue and its followers to declare the Eritrean movements, which enjoyed revolutionary credentials during the monarchy, as "foreign-instigated" and "feudalist" and which had to be opposed for the sake of the "unity of the proletarian struggle."

In Nigeria, the South opposed in principle the North's wish to secede in the 1950s and denounced it as serving the colonialists. When the (South) East seceded, the North fought the secession as "neocolonialist" and "balkanizing." Nkrumah's Ghana opposed Togolese irredentism and Ewe separatism but, at the same time, called on the Ewe in Togo to unite with Ghana. Nkrumah was opposed to tribalist federalism in Ghana, but saw nothing wrong in active support for Agni separatism in the Ivory Coast and publicly voicing his sympathies for the secessionists in Eritrea, Southern Sudan, the Ogaden, and the NFD. Zaire fought the secession of Katanga, but it also fought *for* the secession of the Cabinda enclave from neighboring Angola. Uganda suppressed the separatism of Buganda and Rwenzururu, but intermittently supported the Southern Sudanese Anyanya and was close to recognizing Biafra. It seems that not only has every state its own Katanga, but every Katanga has its own Congo-Brazzaville (which supported Katanga).

Morocco insisted on self-determination by plebiscite in the Western Sahara as long as it thought it might lead to reunification. Since it has become apparent that the Saharwi may opt for independence, Morocco has opposed a truly free plebiscite. For Morocco's opponents, the transfer of Ifni to Morocco by the Spanish-Moroccan Treaty of Fez in 1969 was seen as implementing self-determination and decolonization. The same procedure applied in 1976 in the Treaty of Madrid to the Western Sahara was denounced as denial of self-determination and colonization.

Radical states opposed conservative secessions (e.g., Katanga, Buganda,

Southern Sudan) as reactionary and imperialistic, though often sympathizing with revolutionary separatists (e.g., Somalis, Eritreans, Saharwi). Conservative governments did the reverse. When the Ethiopian and Somali governments switched sides in the global East-West competition between 1977 and 1978, the pro-Soviet supporters of the Somali and Eritrean secessionists became their fierce opponents while their previous enemies of before became their staunchest supporters.

The secessionists are no better than the governments. Every secessionist movement insists that it is a special case, that the dominoes will only fall with the secession of somebody else. The Somalis insist that they are the only true nation-state and that Ethiopia is the last colonial power. The Eritreans insist that they were a colony which should not have become a part of Ethiopia. The Biafrans invoked the danger of genocide, the Katangans the communist threat, and the Southern Sudanese the memories of the slave trade and Arab imperialism. Cabinda was an enclave, Mayotte an island, and Buganda a kingdom. Secessionists, who fight against the principle of territorial integrity of the state as a whole, insist on the territorial integrity of the seceding region. And if the Baluba in Katanga, the Ijaw in Biafra, the Rendille in the NFD, or the Kunama in Eritrea do not want secession, the secessionist governments and movements follow Rousseau and try to force them to be free.

African leaders and governments who demanded international intervention and supported the use of force in order to liberate colonies or fight the white minority regimes in the name of the right of national self-determination, barricaded themselves against similar interventions by sanctifying the principles of noninterference and territorial integrity. Support for the national self-determination of Angola's and South Africa's African majority was legitimate, but the same did not apply to the Ogadenees, Ibos, Eritreans, and Burundi's Hutus.

10

SUMMARY AND CONCLUSION

In Africa, like anywhere else, the principle of national self-determination is open to many and conflicting interpretations. While, in the 1940s and 1950s, it meant democratic participation in Francophone Africa and a combination of independence with democracy in Anglophone Africa, it has shifted since the 1960s to mean external freedom rather than national self-government. The switch from democratic determination to national determinism resembles what happened in Eastern Europe after World War I.

Critical concepts are the different interpretations of the national self. The dominant self is the colonial self, although it is, in most cases, hardly national and even lacks an ethnonational core. An important observation is that some kind of colonial self enjoys the legitimacy not only of the statists, but also of the separatists, irredentists, and ethnicists. Quite frequently, the conflict is between peoples and leaders who all claim to represent a different colonial self. Other selves, which sometimes compete and clash with the colonial self, are the ethnocultural nation, the historic state, the natural geographic unit, and the communal group which claims a heterogeneous territory for one homogeneous group. Almost all conflicts in Africa can be explained as a clash between different national selves.

Very often, the perception of peoples as natives or settlers is crucial. National self-determination is usually denied to those regarded as foreign intruders. The critical date, often in dispute between the parties to the conflict, decides when a settler becomes a legitimate national to be accorded the right to belong and the right to determine.

Independence is the most common goal of self-determination, although in Africa as elsewhere there have been exceptions to this rule. The means to the implementation of national self-determination have been even more numerous than the goals. They include plebiscites; decisions by semi-independent, regional, and traditional governments; general elections and parliamentary votes; reports by investigation commissions; armed struggle by guerilla movements; and nomadic self-determination by emigration. The forms of self-determination fall into two broad categories—self-determination from above by elites and oligarchies and self-determination from below by elections and mass movements.

In Africa, we witness a repeat performance of the European nineteenth century debate as to whether the right to national self-determination does or does not contain the right to secede. The African establishment, represented by the OAU and the official governments, denies any connection between self-determination and secession. Sometimes, it regards self-determination as local self-government rather than independence. Other ways of rejecting secession without challenging the legitimacy of national self-determination are by denationalizing the peoples involved and denying the representativeness of the secessionists. The secessionists, for their part, certainly see the right to self-determination and the right to secede as synonymous. Opposition to secession is not as total and consistent as claimed in the literature on contemporary Africa. The case studies discussed in this volume demonstrate that every secession had its supporters and that state interests and dramatic events may lead to a sudden collapse of the status quo ideology.

Because there exists an African consensus that only anticolonial self-determination is legitimate and worthy of support, the definition of what colonial means becomes an important issue. Anticolonial nationalism of the 1940s and 1950s defined colonial according to the salt water theory, the pigmentational logic, and the continental origin of rulers and ruled. Since the 1960s, there is definitely an increase in the use of the concept of colonialism by Africans against Africans. The notion of internal colonialism imported from Europe and America may lead to a renewed destabilization of the conservative state system.

Another classical issue discussed is the question of the optimal size of states for the purpose of self-determination. Different perceptions of key concepts like viability, balkanization, and domino theory illustrate the debate between those who favor big states and those who want a world composed of small communities.

In Africa, the principle of national self-determination has also frequently collided with other international norms and values. The most important normative competitors of national self-determination are the territorial integrity of states, the states' right to self-defense, the peaceful resolution of conflict, noninterference in the internal affairs of sovereign states, and international peace and security.

A final chapter has dealt with the double standard in the application of national self-determination. The double standard characterized the policies and attitudes of governments and secessionist movements, of Muslim-Arab and Christian-African states and of radical and conservative rulers. All were flexible in interpreting the principle of national self-determination in a way that would suit their personal, group, or state interests. In that sense, they were no different from Revolutionary France, czarist Russia, Woodrow Wilson's America, communist China, or Nehru's India.

The analysis of the concept of self-determination and its use in Africa has provided us with a theoretical framework which clarifies many of Africa's postcolonial interethnic conflicts, border disputes, secessions, and irredentist wars. It certainly is not a substitute for a thorough empirical study of each conflict, but we think it offers an important additional perspective. This study should also enable us to abandon a narrow regionalist approach and, hence, perceive Africa's problems in a universal and comparative perspective. Substantially, the problem of national self-determination is a universal one. The debate on the proper definition and interpretation of national self-determination resembles similar debates elsewhere. The same is true with regard to the basic dilemmas inherent in the concept of self-determination: What is the self? What is determined? How is self-determination implemented? What is the connection between the right of self-determination and the right of secession? What is the optimal size of a viable state? Is self-determination reversible? Does it conflict with other international principles? With regard to the double standard, we do not need to put a question mark. It is alive and well in Africa, as anywhere else in this imperfect world.

NOTES

Introduction

1. R. Lansing as quoted by M. Pomerance, *Self-Determination in Law and Practice* (The Hague: Martinus Nijhoff Publishers, 1982), p. 74.
2. R. Lansing as quoted by A. Cobban, *The Nation State and National Self-Determination* (New York: Thomas Crowell Company, 1970), p. 62.
3. M. Walzer, *Just and Unjust Wars—A Moral Argument with Historical Illustrations* (New York: Basic Books, 1977), p. xiii.

Chapter 1

1. W. Wilson quoted by S. Wambaugh, *Plebiscites Since the World War* (Washington, Carnegie Endowment for International Peace, 1933), p. 11.
2. C.A. MaCartney, *National States and National Minorities* (London, Oxford University Press, 1934), p. 47.
3. W. Ofuatey-Kodjoe, *The Principle of Self-Determination in International Law* (New York: Nellen Publishing Company, 1977), p. xii.
4. P. Calvert, "On Attaining Sovereignty" in A. Smith, ed., *Nationalist Movements* (London: Macmillan Press, 1976), p. 148.
5. K. Rabl, *Das Selbstbestimmungsrecht der Völker—Geschichtliche Grundlagen und Umriss der gegenwärtigen Bedeutung* (Koln: Bohlau Verlag, 1973), p. 5.
6. E. Kedourie, *Nationalism* (New York: Praeger, 1960), pp. 20–31.
7. E. Burke as quoted by A. Cobban, p. 32.
8. M.C. McEwen, *International Boundaries in East Africa* (Oxford: The Clarendon Press, 1970), pp. 31–32.
9. R. Emerson, *Self-Determination Revisited in the Era of Decolonization* (Cambridge: Center for International Affairs, Harvard University, 1964), p. 27.
10. Z. Cervenka, *The Unfinished Quest for Unity—Africa and the OAU* (London: Friedman, 1977).
11. J. Plamenatz, *On Alien Rule and Self-Government* (London: Longmans, 1960), p. 2.
12. PAFMECA Freedom Charter in T. Mboya, *Freedom and After* (Boston: Little Brown, 1963), p. 92.
13. S. Touré, *L'Afrique et la révolution* (Paris: Présence Africaine, n.d.), p. 33.

14. M. Pomerance, p. 1.

15. J. Faust, "Self-Determination: A Definitional Focus" in Y. Alexander and A. Friedlander, eds., *Self-Determination—National, Regional and Global Dimensions* (Boulder: Westview Press, 1980), p. 13.

16. D. Ronen, *The Quest for Self-Determination* (New Haven: Yale University Press, 1979), p. 22.

17. Lung-chu Chen, "Self-Determination as a Human Right" in M. Reisman and B.H. Weston, eds., *Toward World Order and Human Dignity* (New York: The Free Press, 1976), p. 216.

18. Y. Faust, p. 6.

19. On the distinction between "Staatsnation" and "Kulturnation," see F. Meinecke, *Weltbürgertum und Nationalstaat* (München: Oldenburg Verlag, 1928).

20. A.D. Smith, *Nationalism in the Twentieth Century* (Oxford: Robertson, 1979), p. 13.

Chapter 2

1. J.S. Mill, *Considerations on Representative Government* (Indianapolis: Library of Liberal Arts Press, 1958), p. 232.

2. C.A. MaCartney, p. 16.

3. J. Plamenatz, p. 1.

4. Y. Dinstein, "Self-Determination and the Middle East Conflict" in Y. Alexander and A. Friedlander, p. 243.

5. J. Rothschild, *Ethno-politics—A Conceptual Framework (New York: Columbia University Press, 1981), p. 14.*

6. H.S. Johnson and B. Singh, "Self-Determination and World Order" in Y. Alexander and A. Friedlander, p. 354.

7. H. Kohn, *The Idea of Nationalism—A Study in Its Origins and Background* (New York: Collier, 1967).

8. E. Kedourie, p. 132.

9. U.O. Umozurike, *Self-Determination in International Law* (n.p.: Archon Books, 1972), pp. 18–19.

10. J. Plamenatz, p. 17.

11. D. Ronen, p. 23.

12. H. Kohn as quoted by D. Ronen, p. 27.

13. D. Ronen, p. 65.

14. H. Kloss, *Grundfragen der Ethnopolitik im 20. Jahrhundert* (Bad Godesberg: Verlag Wissenschaftliches Archiv, 1969), p. 461.

15. E.H. Carr, *Conditions for Peace* (New York: MacMillan, 1942), p. 39.

16. J. Plamenatz, p. 1.

17. J.S. Mill, pp. 229–237.

18. J. Nyerere quoted by K. Rabl, p. 492.

Chapter 3

1. I. Jennings, *An Approach to Self-Government* (Boston: Beacon Press, 1963), p. 56.

2. E. Kedourie, p. 9.

3. K. Kaunda, *A Humanist in Africa* (London: Longmans, 1969), p. 82.

4. F. Youlou quoted by C. Young, *The Politics of Cultural Pluralism* (Madison: The University of Wisconsin Press, 1976), p. 185.

5. A. Smith, *Nationalist Movements*, p. 3.

6. M. Pomerance, p. 73.

7. F. Hertz, *Nationality in History and Politics—A Psychology and Sociology of National Sentiment and Nationalism* (London: Routledge and Kegan Paul, 1957), pp. 186–7; *Nationalism—A Report by a Study Group of Members of the Royal Institute of International Affairs* (New York: Kelley, 1966), pp. 118–125.

8. A.D. Smith, *Nationalism in the Twentieth Century,* p. 42.

9. A. Mazrui and M. Tidy, *Nationalism and New States in Africa* (Nairobi: Heinemann, 1984), p. 125.

10. A. Mazrui and M. Tidy, p. xviii.

11. T. Hodges, *Western Sahara—The Roots of a Desert War* (Westport, Conn.: Lawrence Hill, 1983), p. 134.

12. W. Ofuatey-Kodjoe, pp. 183–184.

13. E. Mortimer, *France and the Africans 1944–1960—A Political History* (New York: Walker and Company, 1969), pp. 99, 105, 267.

14. M. Keita as quoted by V. Matthies, *Der Grenzkonflikt Somalias mit Äthiopien und Kenya* (Hamburg: Institut fur Afrikakunde, 1977), p. 327.

15. S. Touré, interview in *Jeune Afrique,* June 30, 1968.

16. J. Mayall, "Self-Determination and the OAU" in I.M. Lewis, ed., *Nationalism and Self-Determination in the Horn of Africa* (London: Ithaca Press, 1983), p. 91.

17. R. Johannét quoted in B. Shafer, *Nationalism: Myth and Reality* (London: Gollancz, 1955), p. 62.

18. I.M. Lewis, "Pre- and Post-Colonial Forms of Polity in Africa" in I.M. Lewis, ed., p. 74.

19. Ethiopia's Prime Minister Aklilu Habte Wäld in B. Boutros-Ghali, *Les conflits des frontiers en Afrique* (Paris: Editions Techniques et Economiques, 1972), p. 107.

20. V. Matthies, *Der Grenzkonflikt Somalias mit Äthiopien und Kenya,* p. 54.

21. V. Matthies, *Der Grenzkonflikt Somalias mit Äthiopien und Kenya,* p. 83.

22. V. Matthies, *Der Eritrea Konflikt—Ein Vergessener Krieg am Horn von Afrika* (Hamburg: Institut fur Afrikakunde, 1981), p. 61.

23. O. Arikpo, *The Development of Modern Nigeria* (Baltimore: Penguin, 1967), p. 13.

24. Haile-Selassie as quoted by the *New York Times,* January 19, 1971.

25. A.G.A.A. Ghaffar, *Politische Integration und Desintegration in einem Entwicklungsland—Dargestellt am Beispiel des Regionalen Konflikts in der Republik Sudan Zwishen 1946–1969* (Frankfurt A.M.: Haag Herchen, 1979), p. 116.

26. R.F. Nyrop et al., *Area Handbook for Rwanda* (Washington: U.S. Government, 1969), p. 21.

27. R. Lemarchand, *Rwanda and Burundi* (New York: Praeger, 1970), p. 86.

28. On the historical background of Eritrea, see H. Erlich, *The Struggle Over Eritrea—War and Revolution in the Horn of Africa* (Stanford: Hoover Institution Press, 1983).

29. B. Davidson, "An Historical Note" in B. Davidson, L. Cliffe, and B.H. Selassie, eds., *Behind the War in Eritrea* (Nottingham: Russel Press, 1980), p. 12.

30. B. Davidson, p. 12.

31. J. Damis, *Conflict in Northwest Africa—The Western Sahara Dispute* (Stanford: Hoover Institution Press, 1983), p. 43.

32. S. Touval, *Boundary Politics in Africa* (Cambridge: Harvard University Press, 1972), p. 23; *West Africa* (September 16, 1961 and August 15, 1970), p. 925; S. Touval,

"The Sources of the Status Quo and Irredentist Politics" in C.G. Widstrand, *African Boundary Problems* (Stockholm: Almquist and Widsell, 1969), pp. 110, 114; *Afrique Nouvelle* (September 20, 1961).

33. S. Cronje, *The World and Nigeria* (London: Sidgwick and Jackson, 1972), p. 291.

34. V. Levine, "The Politics of Partition in Africa," *Journal of International Affairs* 18, no. 2 (1964): p. 203. Various African conferences accepted resolutions in support of the movement: see S. Touval, *Boundary Politics in Africa*, pp. 42, 48.

35. D. Brown, "Borderline Politics in Ghana—the National Liberation Movement of Western Togoland," *Journal of Modern African Studies* 18, no. 4 (1980): pp. 575–609. See also N. Chasan, *An Anatomy of Ghanaian Politics* (Boulder: Westview Press, 1983), pp. 236–237.

36. S. Healy, "The Changing Idiom of Self-Determination in the Horn of Africa" in I.M. Lewis, ed., p. 103.

37. B. Boutros-Ghali, p. 113.

38. Quoted by C. Phillips, "Nigeria and Biafra" in F.L. Shiels, ed., *Ethnic Separatism and World Politics,* (Lanham: University Press of America, 1984), p. 176.

39. D.M. Wai, "Geoethnicity and the Margin of Autonomy in the Sudan" in D. Rothchild and V.A. Oluronsola eds., *State Versus Ethnic Claims—African Policy Dilemmas* (Boulder: Westview Press, 1983), pp. 304–330.

40. B. Malwal, *People and Power in the Sudan—The Struggle for National Stability* (London: Ithaca Press, 1981), pp. 21–22.

41. D.C. Mulford, *Zambia—The Politics of Independence 1957–1964* (Oxford: Oxford University Press, 1967).

42. M. Newitt, *The Comoro Islands—Struggle Against Dependency in the Indian Ocean* (Boulder: Westview Press, 1984); J. Ostheimer, *The Politics of the Western Indian Ocean Islands* (New York: Praeger, 1975), pp. 73–101.

43. M. Newitt, p. 56.

44. D.D. Santos, "Cabinda: The Politics of Oil in Angola's Enclave" in R. Cohen, ed., *African Islands and Enclaves,* (Beverly Hills: Sage Publications, 1983), pp. 102–106.

45. J. Damis, p. 107; T. Hodges, p. 95.

46. B. Neuberger, *Involvement, Invasion and Withdrawal—Qaddafi's Libya and Chad 1969–1981* (Tel Aviv: Shiloah Center for Middle Eastern and African Studies, 1982).

47. E. Mortimer, p. 359.

48. J. Rothschild, *Ethnopolitics,* p. 6.

49. A. Smith, *Theories of Nationalism* (New York: Harper and Row, 1971).

50. A. Smith, *The Ethnic Revival in the Modern World* (Cambridge: Cambridge University Press, 1981), p. xii.

51. A. Lijphart, *Democracy in Plural Societies: A Comparative Exploration* (New Haven: Yale University Press, 1977), p. 28.

52. E. Nordlinger, *Conflict Regulation in Divided Societies* (Cambridge: Harvard University Center of International Affairs, 1972), p. 12.

53. A.G.A.A. Ghaffar, p. 116.

54. K. Minogue, *Nationalism* (London: Batsford, 1967), p. 13.

55. R. Greenfield, "Pre-colonial and Colonial History" in B. Davidson, L. Cliffe, and B.H. Selassie, eds., p. 17.

56. T. Turner, "Congo Kinshasa" in V. Oluronsola, ed., *The Politics of Cultural Subnationalism in Africa* (Garden City: Doubleday, 1972), p. 208; R. Lemarchand, "The Bases of Nationalism among the Bakongo", *Africa,* no. 4 (Winter 1961): pp. 344–354.

57. B.H. Selassie, *Conflict and Intervention in the Horn of Africa* (New York: Monthly Review Press, 1980), p. 83.

58. R. Lemarchand, "The State and Society in Africa: Ethnic Stratification and Re-stratification in Historical and Comparative Perspective" in D. Rothchild and V.A. Oluronsola, eds., p. 50.

59. C.S. Phillips, p. 158.

60. B. Akinyemi, "Nigeria and Fernando Poo—The Politics of Irredentism," *African Affairs* 69, no. 276 (July 1970): pp. 236–249.

61. V. Levine, *The Cameroon Federal Republic* (Ithaca: Cornell University Press, 1971), p. 16.

62. Z. Cervenka, p. 70.

63. D. Austin, "The Uncertain Border: Ghana-Togo," *Journal of Modern African Studies* 1, no. 2 (1963): pp. 139–145.

64. D. Brown, p. 548.

65. M. Newitt, p. 28; J. Ostheimer, pp. 72–101.

66. J. Damis, p. 54; T. Hodges, pp. 100–102.

67. V. Matthies, *Der Grenzkonflikt Somalias mit Äthiopien und Kenya,* p. 73.

68. H.M. Adam, "Language, National Consciousness and Identity—The Somali Experience" in I.M. Lewis, ed., p. 31.

69. C. Legum, "Somali Liberation Songs," *Journal of Modern African Studies* 1, no. 4 (1963): pp. 503–519.

70. *Africa Report* 26, nos. 5–6 (May-June 1981): pp. 12–14.

71. B. Boutros-Ghali, p. 4.

72. P. Gilkes, "Centralism and the Ethiopian PMAC" in I.M. Lewis, ed., p. 211.

73. R. Tholomier, *Djibouti—Pawn in the Horn of Africa* (Metuchen: Scarecrow Press, 1981), p. 134.

74. B. Malwal, pp. 34–35.

75. J. Oduho and W. Deng, *The Problem of the Southern Sudan* (London: Oxford University Press, 1963), p. 63.

76. B. Malwal, p. 15.

77. B.H. Selassie, p. 109.

78. I.M. Lewis, "The Western Somali Liberation Front (WSLF) and the Legacy of Sheikh Hussein of Bale" in J. Tubiana ed., *Modern Ethiopia—From the Accession of Menelik to the Present* (Rotterdam: Balkema 1980), p. 409.

79. A. Mazrui and M. Tidy, p. 161.

80. K. Nkrumah quoted by C. Legum, *Pan Africanism—A Short Political Guide* (New York: Praeger, 1965), p. 43.

81. K. Nkrumah, *Class Struggle in Africa* (New York: International Publishers, 1970), p. 66; K. Nkrumah, *Handbook of Revolutionary Warfare* (London: Panaf Books, 1968), p. 46; T. Mboya, *Freedom and After* (Boston: Little Brown, 1963), pp. 109, 211; T. Mboya, *Challenge of Nationhood* (London: Heinemann, 1970), pp. 45–46; J. Nyerere, *Freedom and Unity—Uhuru na Umoja* (Dar es Salaam: Oxford University Press, 1966), p. 43; J. Kenyatta, *Harambee—The Prime Minister of Kenya's Speeches 1963–1964* (Nairobi: Oxford University Press, 1964), p. 110; O. Ojukwu, *Biafra II—Random Thoughts* (New York: Harper and Row, 1969), p. xvii.

82. The same tolerance is not accorded to some more recent immigrants who migrated to neighboring countries in the colonial or postcolonial period (e.g., Kenya-Luos in Uganda, Mossi in Ghana, Ghanaians in Nigeria). Nevertheless, nobody refutes their "Africanness," even though they are not accepted in the projected Ugandan, Ghanaian, or Nigerian nation.

83. A.J. Halbach, *Die Südafrikanischeh Bantu Homelands—Konzeption, Struktur, Entwicklungsperspektiven* (München: Weltforum, 1975).

84. M. Barres as quoted by C. Hayes, *Historical Evolution of Modern Nationalism* (New York: McMillan, 1948), p. 192.

85. See, for example, H.V. Treitschke, *Politics* (New York: Harcourt, Brace and World Company, 1968).

86. E. Rénan quoted by F. Hertz, p. 28.

87. A. Smith, ed., *Nationalist Movements*, p. 3.

88. B. Shafer, pp. 25–26 (Hegel); S. Bloom, *The World of Nations—National Implications in the Works of Karl Marx* (New York: AMS Press, 1967), pp. 43–45; Lord Acton, "Nationality," in Lord Acton, *Essays on Freedom and Power* (New York: Meridian, 1965), pp. 141–170.

89. S. Avineri, "Afro-Asia and the Western Political Tradition," *Parliamentary Affairs* 15, no. 1 (Winter 1962): pp. 58–73.

90. An example of the kind of anticolonial nationalism which aims to prove Africa's greatness vis-à-vis Europe is Cheikh Anta Diop's *L'unité culturelle de l'Afrique noire* (Paris: Présence Africaine, 1959).

91. O.K. Dike as quoted in R. Emerson, *From Empire to Nation* (Boston: Beacon Press, 1968), p. 154.

92. P. Curtin, "Nationalism in Africa 1945–1965," *Review of Politics* 28, no. 2, (April 1966): pp. 143–153.

93. D. Rustow, *A World of Nations—Problems of Political Modernization* (Washington: The Brooking Institution, 1967), p. 40.

94. S. Touval, *Boundary Politics in Africa,* p. 7.

95. R. Lemarchand, "The Bases of Nationalism Among the Bakongo," p. 347; T. Turner, p. 210.

96. Albert Kalonji was crowned as Mulopwe of South Kasai; Mulopwe was the traditional designation of the Luba kings.

97. A.H.M. Kirk-Greene ed., *Crisis and Conflict in· Nigeria—A Documentary Sourcebook 1966–1969* 2 (London: Oxford University Press, 1971), p. 7.

98. J. Oduho and W. Deng, p. 59.

99. D. Wai, "Geoethnicity and the Margin of Autonomy in the Sudan" in D. Rothchild and V. Oluronsola, ed., p. 309.

100. A. Jaden quoted by B. Malwal, p. 100.

101. O. Ojukwu, *Biafra II,* p. 2.

102. B.H. Selassie, *Conflict and Intervention in the Horn of Africa,* passim.

103. B.H. Selassie, "From British Rule to Federation and Annexation" in B. Davidson, L. Cliffe, and B.H. Selassie, eds., *Behind the War in Eritrea,* p. 32.

104. B.H. Selassie, "From British Rule to Federation and Annexation", p. 33.

105. Abdirizak Haji Hussein, Radio Magadisho, September 19, 1966; Abdi Rashid Shermarke, Radio Omdurman, April 4, 1968; Mohammed Ibrahim Egal, quoted in *Africa Report* 14, 1 (January 1969): p. 25.

106. Mesfin Wolde Mariam, "The Background of the Ethio-Somalian Dispute," *Journal of Modern African Studies* 2, 2 (1964): p. 193.

107. V. Matthies, *Der Eritrea Konflikt,* pp. 10–11.

108. S. Healy, p. 98.

109. H. Erlich, pp. 12, 49.

110. *Ethiopia Observer,* September 16, 1966.

111. M. Reisman, "Somali Self-Determination in the Horn—Legal Perspectives and Implications for Social and Political Engineering" in I.M. Lewis ed., p. 153.

112. Mesfin Wolde Mariam, p. 217.

113. Radio Blantyre, September 21, 1968.

114. T. Hodges, pp. 85–91.

115. S. Touval, *Boundary Politics in Africa,* p. 35.

116. T. Hodges, pp. 25–27, 80; J. Damis, pp. 11–12, 21–29.

117. M. Dia, *The African Nations and World Solidarity* (New York: Praeger, 1961), p. 108.

118. L.S. Senghor, *On African Socialism* (New York: Praeger, 1964), p. 84.

119. W. Foltz, *From French West Africa to the Mali Federation* (New Haven: Yale University Press, 1965), p. 144.

120. C. Welch, *Dream of Unity—Pan Africanism and Political Integration in West Africa* (Ithaca: Cornell University Press, 1966), p. 349.

121. J. Nyerere, *Freedom and Unity*, pp. 291–292.

122. C. Welch, p. 278; S. Touré, *Doctrine and Methods of the Democratic Party of Guinea* (n.p., n.d.), p. 131.

123. E. Kedourie, *Nationalism in Asia and Africa* (New York: The World Publishing Company, 1970), p. 36.

124. E. Kedourie, *Nationalism in Asia and Africa,* p. 50.

125. Malawi demanded, in the 1960s, parts of Zambia and Tanzania which were taken away by the colonial partition. In 1974, it raised demands to parts of Mozambique.

126. A. Smith, *Theories of Nationalism,* p. 22.

127. See, for example, A.J. Shelton, "'The Black Mystique'—Reactionary Extremes in 'Négritude,'" *African Affairs* 63, no. 25 (April 1964): pp. 115–127.

128. A. Smith, *Theories of Nationalism,* p. 22.

129. T. Hodgkin, *Nationalism in Colonial Africa* (New York: New York University Press, 1965), p. 179.

130. J. Nyerere, *Freedom and Unity,* p. 147.

131. J. Nyerere, "A United States of Africa," *Journal of Modern African Studies* 1, no. 1 (Spring 1963): p. 6.

132. J. Touré, *Guinean Revolution and Social Progress* (Cairo: Societé Orientale de Publicité, 1963), pp. 400; K. Nkrumah, *Class Struggle in Africa,* p. 9.

133. *Jeune Afrique,* October 30, 1966 (interview with L. Senghor).

134. L. Senghor, "Négritude et civilisation de l'universel" *Présence Africaine* 46 (1963), p. 10.

135. N. Azikiwe, "Pan Africanism," in R. Emerson and M. Kilson, eds., *The Political Awakening of Africa* (Englewood Cliffs: Prentice Hall, 1965), p. 150.

136. *Ghana Today,* November 23, 1960.

137. D. Rothchild, *Politics of Integration—An East African Documentary* (Nairobi: East African Publishing House, 1968), p. 115.

138. C. Young, "Comparative Claims to Political Sovereignty—Biafra, Katanga, Eritrea" in D. Rothchild and V.A. Oluronsola, eds., p. 220.

139. *Dalka* 11, no. 1 (July 1, 1966): p. 17.

140. R. Um Nyobe as quoted in R. Emerson, p. 129.

141. Gandhi once said "we were one nation before they came to India," (E. Kedourie, *Nationalism in Asia and Africa,* p. 60) although British conquest was as easy as it was because of the high degree of fragmentation on the Indian subcontinent. Ferhat Abbas spoke about the "revival" of the Algerian nation (D. Gordon, *Self-Determination and History in the Third World* (Princeton: Princeton University Press, 1971, p. 34) although it never existed prior to the French conquest.

142. K. Nkrumah, "Handbook for Revolutionary Warfare," *Dark Days in Ghana* (New York: International Publishers, 1969), p. 25.

143. A. Mazrui, "On the Concept 'We are all Africans,'" *American Political Science Review* 58, no. 1 (March 1963): p. 89.

144. L.S. Senghor, *On African Socialism,* p. 92.

145. M. Dia, p. 10.

146. J. Nyerere, "Tanganayika Today—A Nationalist View," *International Affairs* 36, no. 1 (January 1960): p. 44.

147. F. Rénan as quoted in R. Emerson, p. 149.

148. B. Neuberger, "What is a Nation?—A Contribution to the Debate on the Palestinian Question," *State, Government and International Relations* (Hebrew University), no. 9 (May 1976): pp. 90–108. (Hebrew)

149. I.M. Lewis, *The Modern History of Somaliland—From Nation to State* (New York: Praeger, 1965), p. 161.

150. L. Silberman, "Change and Conflict in the Horn of Africa," *Foreign Affairs,* 37, no. 4 (October 1958): pp. 649–660.

151. A. Enahoro as quoted by C.S. Phillips, p. 176.

152. E. Kedourie, *Nationalism in Asia and Africa,* p. 28.

153. N. Azikiwe, *Zik—A Selection from the Speeches of Nnamdi Azikiwe* (Cambridge: Cambridge University Press, 1961), p. 121.

154. J. Kenyatta, *Suffering Without Bitterness—The Founding of the Kenya Nation* (Nairobi: East African Publishing House, 1968), pp. 211–215.

155. H. Kohn, *Nationalism—Its Meaning and History* (New York: Van Nostrand, 1965), p. 6.

156. R. Tholomier, pp. 4–5, 40–41.

157. V. Matthies, *Der Grenzkonflikt Somalias mit Äthiopien und Kenya,* p. 83.

158. M. Pomerance, p. 2.

159. H. Erlich, pp. 19–20.

160. T. Hodges, p. 150.

161. D. Ronen, p. 13.

162. D. Ronen, p. 94.

Chapter 4

1. Lung-chu Chen, p. 237.

2. A.D. Smith, *Nationalism in the Twentieth Century,* p. 3.

3. P. Calvert, p. 48.

4. M. Pomerance, p. 12.

5. J. Ostheimer, p. 181.

6. A.R. Sureda, *The Evolution of the Right of Self-Determination—A Study of United Nations Practice* (Leiden, A.W. Sijthoff, 1973), p. 51.

7. "The Declaration to Solve the Problem in Eritrea in a Peaceful Way" (Addis Ababa, May 16, 1976), quoted in O. Gilkes, p. 197.

8. V. Matthies, *Der Grenzkonflikt Somalias mit Äthiopien und Kenya,* p. 75.

9. T. Hodges, p. 212.

10. V. Matthies, *Der Eritrea Konflikt,* p. 63.

11. J. Rothschild, p. 153.

Chapter 5

1. R. Emerson, "Self-Determination Revisted in the Era of Decolonization," p. 30.

2. A. Cobban, p. 6.

3. S. Huntington quoted by N. Stultz, *Transkei's Half Loaf* (New Haven, Yale

University Press, 1979), p. 4.

4. B.H. Selassie, *Conflict and Intervention in the Horn of Africa*, p. 89.

5. J. Tubiana, "The Linguistic Approach to Self-Determination" in I.M. Lewis, ed., p. 23.

6. H. Beran, "A Liberal Theory of Secession," *Political Studies* 32, no. 1 (1984), p. 23.

7. V.I. Lenin, *The Right of Nations to Self-Determination* (New York: International Publishers, 1951), p. 112.

8. See, for example, O. Bauer, *Die Nationalitätenfrage und Sozialdemokratie* (Wien: Volksbuchhandlung, 1924), p. 291.

9. V.I. Lenin as quoted in W. Connor, *The National Question in Marxist— Leninist Theory and Strategy* (Princeton: Princeton University Press, 1984), p. 40.

10. F. Halliday and M. Molyneux, *The Ethiopian Revolution* (London: Verso 1981), p. 168.

11. R. Emerson, "The Problem of Identity, Selfhood and Image in New Nations—The Situation in Africa," *Comparative Politics* (April 1969): p. 300.

12. M.C. McEwen, p. 33.

13. J.F. Murphy, "Self-Determination—United States Perspectives" in Y. Alexander and A. Friedlander eds., pp. 45–46.

14. L.C. Buchheit, *Secession—The Legitimacy of Self-Determination* (New Haven: Yale University Press, 1978), p. 30.

15. J. Mayall, p. 89.

16. R. Jackson and C. Rosberg, "Why Africa's Weak States Persist—The Empirical and the Juridicial in Statehood," *World Politics* 35, no. 1 (October 1982): pp. 1–24.

17. C.J. Friedrich, *Man and His Government* (New York: McGraw-Hill, 1963), p. 565.

18. A. Lijphart, pp. 44–45.

19. C.C. O'Brien, "The Right to Secede," *New York Times,* December 30, 1971.

20. M. Walzer, p. 93.

21. J. Forbes, "Do Tribes Have Rights—The Question of Self-Determination," *Journal of Human Relations* 18, no. 1 (1970): p. 677.

22. C. Legum, "Somali Liberation Songs," p. 512.

23. A. Mazrui, *Towards a Pax Africana—A Study of Ideology and Ambition* (London: Weidenfeld and Nicolson, 1967), p. 12.

24. A. Ahidjo in *Afrique Nouvelle,* May 16, 1968.

25. M. Dia, pp. 5–6.

26. V. Matthies, *Der Grenzkonflikt Somalias mit Äthiopien und Kenya,* pp. 120–121; J. Kenyatta, "Pan African Nucleus," *Spearhead* 11, no. 2 (February 1962): p. 12; C. Njonjo in M.C. McEwen, p. 35; A. Mazrui, p. 12.

27. Mesfin Wolde Mariam, p. 214.

28. A.H.M. Kirk-Greene, vol. 1, p. 416, and vol. 2, pp. 65, 147, 163, 225, 318.

29. N. Azikiwe, *Zik,* p. 190; N. Azikiwe, "Realities of African Unity," *Africa Forum II,* (1965): pp. 21–22; O. Ojukwu, *Biafra I—Selected Speeches with Journal of Events* (New York: Harper and Row, 1969), passim.

30. O. Arikpo in A.H.M. Kirk-Greene, vol. 2, p. 344.

31. S. Avineri, pp. 58–73.

32. E. Lofoli, "Le principe de l'autodetermination des peuples et des nations et son application en Afrique," *Etudes Congolaises* 12, no. 3 (July-September 1969), p. 25.

33. J. Kenyatta, "Pan African Nucleus," p. 12.

34. J. Drysdale, *The Somali Dispute* (London: Pall Mall, 1964), p. 108.

35. M. Dienne, "Nigerian Patriots Want African Unity," *World Marxist Review* 11,

no. 10 (October 1968): pp. 16–19.

36. A. Enahoro, "Deux milles nations Africaines?," *Jeune Afrique,* October 29, 1969.

37. Y. Gowon in A.H.M. Kirk-Greene, vol. 2, p. 163.

38. T. Otegbeye, "Nigeria and the National Question," *World Marxist Review* 12, no. 10 (October 1969): p. 51.

39. R. Emerson, "The Problem of Identity," p. 300.

40. P.H. Judd, "The Attitudes of the African States toward the Katanga Secession July 1960–January 1963," *Columbia Essays in International Affairs,* 1965.

41. A. Hirshman, "Exit, Voice and the State," *World Politics* 31, no. 1 (October 1978).

42. A. Mazrui, *On Heroes and Uhuru Worship* (London: Longman, 1967), p. 8.

43. B. Malwal, p. 100.

44. D. Wai, p. 305.

45. J. Drysdale, p. 117; Radio Omdurman April 4, 1968; *Africa Report* 16, no. 9 (December 1971): pp. 23–25; *Washington Post,* March 8, 1967; E. Bayne, "The Issue of Greater Somalia," *American University Field Staff Reports* 13, no. 2 (Somalia): p. 8.

46. *Dalka,* 11, no. 3 (September 1, 1966): p. 2.

47. O. Ojukwu, *Biafra I,* p. 143.

48. O. Ojukwu in A.H.M. Kirk-Greene, vol. 1, p. 451.

49. O. Ojukwu, *Biafra I,* p. 332.

50. O. Ojukwu in A.H.M. Kirk-Greene, vol. 2, p. 379.

51. O. Ojukwu, *Biafra I,* p. 7.

52. *Daily Times,* October 20, 1966.

53. A. Bello—The Sarduana of Sokoto, *My Life* (Cambridge: Cambridge University Press, 1962), pp. 118, 133.

54. T.N. Tamuno, "Separatist Agitation in Nigeria since 1914," *Journal of Modern African Studies* 8, no. 4 (1970): pp. 563–584.

55. O. Awolowo, *Awo—The Autobiography of Obafemi Awolowo* (Cambridge: Cambridge University Press, 1960), p. 207.

56. D.A. Ijalaye, "The Civil War and Nigerian Federalism" in A.B. Akinyemi, P.D. Cole, and W. Ofanogoro eds., *Readings on Federalism* (Lagos: Nigerian Institute of International Affairs, 1980), p. 148.

57. N. Azikiwe in A.H.M. Kirk-Greene, vol. 2, p. 18.

58. N. Azikiwe, *Zik,* pp. 114–115.

59. A.H.M. Kirk-Greene, vol. 1, pp. 245–254.

60. C.R. Nixon, "Self-Determination—The Nigeria/Biafra Case," *World Politics* 24, no. 4 (July 1972): pp. 473–497.

61. H. Beran, p. 23.

62. B.H. Selassie, *Conflict and Intervention in the Horn of Africa,* p. 89.

63. D. Wai, pp. 306–309.

64. C. Young, p. 281.

65. Radio Dar es Salaam, September 19, 1968.

66. J. Nyerere quoted by C. Rosberg, "National Identity in African States," *The African Review* 1, 1 (March 1971): p. 83.

67. *The Nationalist,* April 14, 1968.

68. *The Nationalist,* April 4, 1968.

69. *The Nationalist,* April 27, 1968.

70. *The Nationalist,* April 27, 1968.

71. *Afrique Contemporaine,* March 4, 1968, p. 20.

72. F. Houphouet-Boigny quoted in O. Ojukwu, *Biafra I,* p. 228.

73. *The Nationalist,* May 3, 1968.

74. *The Nationalist,* May 21, 1968.

75. *West Africa,* May 10, 1968.

76. G.A. Nweke, *External Intervention in African Conflicts—France and French Speaking Africa in the Nigerian Civil War 1967–1970* (Boston: African Studies Center, Boston University, 1976), pp. 32, 41.

77. S. Cronje, *The World and Nigeria* (London: Sidgwick and Jackson, 1972), pp. 281–319.

78. L.B. Miller, *World Order and Local Disorder—The United Nations and Internal Conflicts* (Princeton: Princeton University Press, 1967), p. 83.

79. S. Touval, *Boundary Politics in Africa,* p. 137.

80. A.J. Klinghoffer, *The Angolan War—A Study in Soviet Policy in the Third World* (Boulder: Westview Press, 1980) p. 58; Z. Cervenka, p. 192.

81. D. Brown, pp. 575–609.

82. A. Triulzi, "Competing Views of National Identity in Ethiopia" in I.M. Lewis ed., p. 113.

Chapter 6

1. M. Hechter, *Internal Colonialism—The Celtic Fringe in British National Development 1536–1966* (London: Routledge and Kegan Paul, 1975), p. 208.

2. W.E.B. DuBois quoted by A. Mazrui and M. Tidy, p. 16.

3. A. Mazrui and M. Tidy, p. 88.

4. I.D. Duchachek quoted by S.M. Finger and G. Singh, "Self-Determination—A United Nations Perspective" in Y. Alexander and A. Friedlander eds., p. 339.

5. Quoted by A. Triulzi, p. 117.

6. D. Ronen, p. 27.

7. R. Emerson, *From Empire to Nation,* p. 307.

8. Lord Hume quoted by M. Pomerance, p. 106.

9. L.C. Chen, p. 223.

10. GAR 1541 (1960) quoted by H. Wiberg, "Self-Determination as an International Issue" in I.M. Lewis ed., p. 48.

11. A. Mazrui, *Towards a Pax Africana,* passim.

12. E. Kedourie, *Nationalism in Asia and Africa,* passim.

13. S. Touval, "The Organisation of African Unity and African Borders," *International Organisation* 21, no. 1 (1967): p. 125.

14. A. Mazrui, *Towards a Pan Africana,* p. 12.

15. Radio Mogadisho, August 3, 1967; November 23, 1966.

16. Quoted by V. Matthies, *Der Grenzkonflikt Somalias mit Äthiopien und Kenya,* p. 338.

17. See the interview with the Somali Minister of Information in *Africa Report* 26, no. 5–6 (May-June 1981): pp. 12–14.

18. *Washington Post,* March 8, 1967.

19. J. Mayall, p. 86.

20. F. Halliday and M. Molyneux, p. 195; T. Bitima and J. Steuber, *Die Ungelöste Nationale Frage in Äthiopien* (Frankfurt: P. Lang, 1983), p. 98.

21. B. Davidson, L. Cliffe, and B.H. Selassie eds., pp. 143–150.

22. B.H. Selassie, "From British Rule to Federation and Annexation," p. 45.

23. R.G. Bhardwaj, *The Dilemma of the Horn of Africa* (New Delhi: Sterling, 1979), pp. 187–189.

24. B.H. Selassie, *Conflict and Intervention in the Horn of Africa,* p. 18.

25. F. Halliday and M. Molyneux, p. 176; P. Baxter, "The Problem of the Oromo or the Problem for the Oromo" in I.M. Lewis, ed., p. 130.

26. P. Baxter, p. 138; R. Léfort, *Ethiopia—An Heretical Revolution* (London: Zed Press, 1983), pp. 36–37.

27. A. Triulzi, p. 123.

28. A. Triulzi, p. 117.

29. A. Triulzi, p. 117.

30. M. DeGarang, "Cairo Union and Southern Sudan," *Grass Curtain* 6, no. 3 (December 1970), p. 4.

31. B. Malwal, pp. 1, 2, 58; D. Wai, pp. 306, 310, 313, 318, 324.

32. J. Okello, *Revolution in Zanzibar* (Nairobi: East African Publishing House, 1967), pp. 72–83.

33. B. Neuberger, *Involvement, Invasion and Withdrawal,* pp. 51–58.

34. Y. Gershoni followed the theme in his book, *Black Colonialism—Americo-Liberian Scramble to the Hinterland* (Boulder: Westview Press, 1985).

35. V. Nanda quoted by L.C. Chen, p. 222.

36. Quoted by A.D. Smith, *Ethnic Revival in the Modern World,* p. 31.

37. M. Hechter, p. 30.

38. S. Carmichael and C. Hamilton, *Black Power—The Politics of Liberation in America* (New York: Random House, 1967).

39. J. Plamenatz, p. 86.

40. J. Plamenatz, p. 86.

41. R.F. Nyrop et al., p. 18.

42. J. Plamenatz, p. 114.

43. D. Wai, p. 307.

44. A. Mazrui, *On Heroes and Uhuru Worship,* p. 165.

Chapter 7

1. I. Wallerstein, *Africa—The Politics of Unity* (New York: Random House, 1961), p. 88.

2. Aklilu Habta-Wäld quoted by Z. Cervenka, p. 9.

3. O. Ojukwu in A.H.M. Kirk-Green, vol. 1, p. 395.

4. S.A. Salim quoted by E. Keller, "The State, Public Policy and the Mediation of Ethnic Conflict in Africa" in D. Rothchild and V. Oluronsola eds., p. 251.

5. H. Beran, p. 25.

6. F. Hertz (Mazzini), pp. 387–392; S. Bloom (Marx), pp. 35–36.

7. F. Hertz, pp. 318–322; H. Kohn, *The Idea of Nationalism,* p. 402.

8. P.W. Blair, *The Ministate Dilemma* (New York: Carnegie Endowment for International Peace, 1967).

9. A.D. Smith, *The Ethnic Revival in the Modern World,* p. 151.

10. L. Buchheit, p. 106.

11. L. Buchheit, p. 5.

12. A. Cobban, p. 65.

13. W.B. Yeats quoted by C. Young, p. 460.

14. R. Dahl and R. Tufte, *Size and Democracy* (Stanford: Stanford University Press, 1973).

15. J. Forbes, pp. 670–679.

16. E. Lemberg, *Nationalisms—Psychologie und Geschichte* (Hamburg: Rowohlt, 1964), p. 177; O. Janowsky, *Nationalities and National Minorities* (New York:

MacMillan, 1945), p. 11.

17. K. Nkrumah, *I Speak for Freedom* (New York: Praeger, 1961), p. 200; *Ghana Today,* June 20, 1962.

18. K. Deutsch, *Nationalism and Its Alternatives* (New York: A. Knopf, 1969), p. 50.

19. Y. Gowon in A.H.M. Kirk-Greene, vol. 2, p. 318.

20. M. Obote in *Uganda Argus,* (Kampala, February 3, 1960). This was said during the Buganda crisis when the Baganda threatened to secede from Uganda.

21. K. Nkrumah, "I Speak for Freedom" in G.C.M. Mutiso and S.W. Rohio eds., *Readings in African Political Thought* (London: Oxford University Press, 1975), p. 214.

22. K. Nkrumah, *I Speak for Freedom,* p. 201.

23. K. Nkrumah in *Ghana Today,* March 10, 1965.

24. A.H.M. Kirk-Greene, vol. 2, p. 225.

25. A. Enahoro in A.H.M. Kirk-Greene, vol. 2, pp. 148, 354.

26. *Daily Nation,* (Nairobi) October 6, l970.

27. V. Matthies, *Der Grenzkonflikt Somalias mit Äthiopien und Kenya,* pp. 244–245.

28. *West Africa,* October 1968, p. 1163.

29. According to D. Mudola ("The Search for the Nation-state and African Peace," *East Africa Journal* (Nairobi) 6, no. 2 (November 1969): pp. 17–22), the creation of Biafra did not encourage other secessions. On the other hand, it is difficult to know what would have happened if Biafra had survived. The Sanwi movement in the Ivory Coast quoted the Biafran precedent, which had been recognised by the government of Houphouet-Boigny. President Macias of Equatorial Guinea said that the Biafran precedent encouraged a secessionist movement in Fernando Poo. Because both movements were much older than the civil war, the role of the precedent is questionable.

30. E. Lemberg, p. 177; O. Janowsky, p. 9; S. Baron, *Modern Nationalities and Religion* (New York: Harper and Brothers, 1947), p. 254.

31. O. Janowsky, p. 9.

32. V.I. Lenin, "Preliminary Draft of Theses in the National and Colonial Questions for the Second Congress of the Communist International, June 5, 1920" in *Collected Works,* vol. 10, (New York: International Publishers, 1938).

33. M. Dia, p. ix; J. Nyerere, *Freedom and Unity,* pp. 40, 137.

34. K. Nkrumah, *Ghana Today,* August 31, 1960.

35. K. Nkrumah, *I Speak for Freedom,* p. 201.

36. K. Nkrumah, *I Speak for Freedom,* p. 255.

37. J. Nyerere, "East African Federation" in G.C.M. Mutiso and S.W. Rohio, eds., p. 337.

38. C. Legum, *Pan Africanism,* p. 274.

39. S. Touré in C. Legum, p. 121.

40. K. Minogue, *Nationalism,* pp. 65–66.

41. G. Buthelezi, "Message to South Africa from Black South Africa," *Soweto,* March 14, 1976.

42. K. Nkrumah, *Class Struggle in Africa,* p. 50; K. Kaunda, *A Humanist in Africa,* p. 123; J. Nyerere, *Freedom and Unity,* pp. 40, 85–6; M. Dia, pp. ix, 84, 140.

43. J. Nyerere, "East African Federation," p. 337.

44. K. Nkrumah, "Continental Government for Africa," p. 345.

45. J. Damis, p. 113.

46. A.G. Gerteiny, "The Racial Factor and Politics in the Islamic Republic of Mauritania," *Race,* (January 1967): pp. 263–275.

47. Haile Selassie in J. Drysdale, p. 100.
48. See W. Foltz, p. 117.
49. E. Mortimer, pp. 238–9.
50. C. Legum, *Pan Africanism,* pp. 273–4.
51. E. Zinsou in *West Africa,* October 5, 1968.
52. A. Bello, p. 118.
53. J. Nyerere, "Why We Recognized Biafra?," *The Observer,* April 28, 1968.
54. O. Ojukwu, *Biafra I,* p. 238.
55. O. Ojukwu, *Biafra I,* p. 238.
56. O. Ojukwu, *Biafra II,* p. 176.
57. O. Ojukwu, *Biafra II,* p. 195.
58. O. Ojukwu, *Biafra II,* p. xx.
59. O.S. Kamanu, "Secession and the Right of Self-Determination—an OAU Dilemma," *Journal of Modern African Studies* 12, no. 3 (1974): pp. 364–367.
60. O.S. Kamanu, p. 360.
61. *Somali Republic and African Unity,* (Nairobi, 1962), pp. 15, 33.
62. M. Pomerance, p. 75.
63. E. Rénan, *Qu'est-ce qu'une nation?* (Paris: Calman Levy, 1882), p. 58.
64. E. Kedourie, *Nationalism,* pp. 62–91.
65. H. Beran, p. 25.
66. H. Kohn, *Nationalism—Its Meaning and History,* passim.
67. D. Wai, p. 315.
68. B. Malwal, p. 100.

Chapter 8

1. W. Wilson quoted by L. Buchheit, p. 63.
2. L. Buchheit, p. 85.
3. Y. El-Ayouty and W. Zartman eds., *The OAU After Twenty Years* (New York: Praeger, 1984), p. 358.
4. UN Resolution 390 A (February 12, 1950) quoted in B. Davidson, L. Cliffe, and B.H. Selassie eds., p. 39.
5. L. Buchheit, p. 86.
6. P. Sigmund, *The Ideologies of Developing Nations* (New York: Praeger, 1965), pp. 104–105.
7. V. Matthies, *Der Grenzkonflikt Somalias mit Äthiopien und Kenya,* p. 43.
8. J. Nyerere quoted by C.C. Mojekwu, "Self-Determination—The African Perspective" in Y. Alexander and R. Friedlander, p. 230.
9. L. Kossuth quoted by C.A. MaCartney, p. 117.
10. P. Tsiranana quoted by V. Matthies, *Der Grenzkonflikt Somalias mit Äthiopien und Kenya,* p. 327.
11. M. Keita quoted by V. Matthies, *Der Grenzkonflikt Somalias mit Äthiopien und Kenya,* p. 327.
12. G.A. Nweke, p. 3.
13. M. Walzer, p. 90.
14. D. Lloyd George quoted by U.O. Umozurike, p. 16.
15. E. Kedouri, *Nationalism in Asia and Africa,* p. 35.
16. W. Ofuatey-Kodjoe, p. xii.

Chapter 9

1. Quoted by C.A. MaCartney, p. 15.
2. R. Kipling quoted by C. Young, p. 505.
3. P.H. Judd, p. 247.
4. J.N. Saxena, *Self-Determination from Biafra to Bangladesh* (Delhi: University of Delhi, 1978), p. 114.
5. L.S. Wiseberg, "Human Rights in Africa—Towards the Definition of the Problem of a Double Standard," *Issue* 6, no. 4 (Winter 1976): p. 5.
6. D. Lloyd-George quoted by U.O. Umozurike, p. 16.
7. R. Emerson quoted by M. Pomerance, p. 61.
8. C.C. Mojekwu, p. 228.
9. C. Hayes, p. 53.
10. K. Rabl, p. 36.
11. C.A. MaCartney, p. 117.
12. S. Bloom, pp. 40–45.
13. V.I. Lenin, "The Right of Nations to Self-Determination," *Selected Works,* vol. 4, (Moscow/Leningrad: Cooperative Publishing Society of Foreign Workers in the USSR, 1935), p. 265.
14. V.I. Lenin, "The National Question in our Programme," *Selected Works,* vol. 2, p. 322.
15. W. Connor, pp. 75, 88, 233–235.
16. W. Connor, pp. 109–110, 116.
17. C.A. MaCartney, p. 182.
18. J. Mayall, p. 88.
19. N. Azikiwe quoted by S. Cronje, p. 287.
20. S. Cronje, p. 284.
21. V. Matthies, *Der Grenzkonflikt Somalias mit Äthiopien und Kenya,* p. 338.
22. V. Matthies, *Der Eritrea Konflikt,* pp. 111–113; R. Léfort, p. 189.
23. W. Ofuatey-Kedjoe, p. 43.
24. Ethiopian Revolutionary Information Center (ERIC) quoted by P. Gilkes, "Centralism and the Ethiopian PMAC" in I.M. Lewis, ed., p. 200.
25. Ethiopian People's Revolutionary Party (EPRP) as quoted in A. Triulzi, p. 14.

BIBLIOGRAPHY

J.E.E.D. Acton. *Essays in Freedom and Power.* New York: Meridian, 1965.

Africa Report 14, no. 1 (January 1969); 16, no. 9 (December 1971), 26, nos. 5–6 (May-June 1981).

Afrique Contemporaine, March 4, 1968.

Afrique Nouvelle, September 22, 1961; May 16, 1968.

B. Akinyemi. "Nigeria and Fernando Poo—The Politics of Irredentism." *African Affairs* 69, no. 276 (July 1970): pp. 236–249.

B. Akinyemi, P.D. Cole, and W. Ofanogoro, eds. *Readings in Federalism.* Lagos: Nigerian Institute of International Affairs, 1980.

Y. Alexander and A. Friedlander eds. *Self-Determination—National, Regional and Global Dimensions.* Boulder: Westview, 1980.

J.C. Anene. *The International Boundaries of Nigeria 1895–1960.* London: Longmans, 1970.

O. Arikpo. *The Development of Modern Nigeria.* Baltimore: Penguin, 1967.

D. Austin. "The Uncertain Border: Ghana-Togo." *Journal of Modern African Studies* 1, no. 2 (1963): pp. 139–145.

S. Avineri. "Afro-Asia and the Western Political Tradition." *Parliamentary Affairs* 15, no. 1 (Winter 1962): pp. 58–73.

O. Awolowo. *Awo—The Autobiography of Obafemi Awolowo.* Cambridge: Cambridge University Press, 1960.

J.A.A. Ayoade. "Federalism in Africa." *Plural Societies* 9, no. 1 (Spring 1978): pp. 3–18.

N. Azikiwe. *Zik—A Selection from the Speeches of Nnamdi Azikiwe.* Cambridge: Cambridge University Press, 1961.

———. "Realities of African Unity." *Africa Forum* 2, no. 1 (1965): pp. 7–72.

S. Baron. *Modern Nationalities and Religion.* New York: Harper and Row, 1947.

O. Bauer. *Die Nationalitätenfrage und Sozialdemokratie.* Wien: Volksbuchhandlung, 1924.

E. Bayne. "The Issue of Greater Somalia." *American University Field Staff Reports* 13, no. 2 (Somalia).

A. Bello-Sardauna of Sokoto. *My Life.* Cambridge: Cambridge University Press, 1962.

H. Beran. "A Liberal Theory of Secession." *Political Studies* 32, no. 1 (1984): pp. 21–31.

R. Bhardwaj. *The Dilemma of the Horn of Africa.* New Delhi: Sterling, 1979.

A. Birch. "Another Liberal Theory of Secession." *Political Studies* 32, no. 4 (1984): pp. 596–602.

T. Bitima and J. Steuber. *Die Ungelöste Nationale Frage in Äthiopien.* Frankfurt: P. Lang, 1983.

P.W. Blair. *The Ministate Dilemma.* New York: Carnegie Endowment for International Peace, 1967.

S. Bloom. *The World of Nations—National Implications in the Works of Karl Marx.* New York: AMS Press 1967.

B. Boutros-Ghali. *Les conflits des frontiers en Afrique.* Paris: Editions Techniques et Economiques, 1972.

D. Brown. "Borderline Politics in Ghana—The National Liberation Movements of Western Togo." *Journal of Modern African Studies.* 18, no. 4 (1980): pp. 575–609.

L.C. Buchheit. *Secession—The Legitimacy of Self-Determination.* New Haven: Yale University Press, 1978.

S. Carmichael and C. Hamilton. *Black Power: The Politics of Liberation in America.* New York: Random House, 1967.

E.H. Carr. *Conditions for Peace.* New York: Macmillan, 1942.

Z. Cervenka. *The Nigerian War 1967–1970.* Frankfurt: Bernard and Graefe, 1971.

———. *The Unfinished Quest for Unity—Africa and the OAU.* London: Friedman, 1977.

N. Chazan. *An Anatomy of Ghanaian Politics.* Boulder: Westview, 1983.

F.D. Chassey. *Mauritanie 1900–1975—de l'ordre colonial à l'ordre neo-colonial entre Maghreb et Afrique Noire.* Paris: Editions anthropos, 1978.

A. Cobban. *The Nation State and National Self-Determination.* New York: Thomas Crowell, 1970.

R. Cohen, ed. *African Islands and Enclaves.* Beverly Hills: Sage, 1983.

W. Connor. *The National Question in Marxist-Leninist Theory and Strategy.* Princeton: Princeton University Press, 1984.

S. Cronje. *The World and Nigeria.* London: Sidgewick and Jackson, 1972.

P. Curtain. "Nationalism in Africa 1945–1965." *Review of Politics* 28, no. 2 (April 1966): pp. 143–153.

R. Dahl and R. Tufte. *Size and Democracy.* Stanford: Stanford University Press, 1973.

Daily Nation (Nairobi), October 6, 1970.

Daily Times (Lagos), October 20, 1966.

Dalka (Mogadisho), July 1, 1966; September 1, 1966.

J. Damis. *Conflict in Northwest Africa—The Western Sahara Dispute.* Stanford: Hoover Institution Press, 1983.

B. Davidson, L. Cliffe, and B.H. Selassie, eds. *Behind the War in Eritrea.* Nottingham: Russel, 1980.

M. DeGarang. "Cairo Union and Southern Sudan." *Grass Curtain* 6, no. 3 (December 1970).

K. Deutsch. *Nationalism and its Alternatives.* New York: A. Knopf, 1969.

M. Dia. *The African Nations and World Solidarity.* New York: Praeger, 1964.

M. Dienne. "Nigerian Patriots Want African Unity." *World Marxist Review* 11, no. 10 (October 1968): pp. 16–19.

C.A. Diop. *L'unité culturelle de l'Afrique noire.* Paris: Présence Africaine, 1959.

J. Drysdale. *The Somali Dispute.* London: Pall Mall, 1964.

Y. El-Ayouty and W. Zartman, eds. *The OAU After Twenty Years.* New York: Praeger, 1984.

R. Emerson. *Self-Determination Revisited in the Era of Decolonization.* Cambridge: Center for International Affairs, Harvard University, 1964.

———. *From Empire to Nation.* Boston: Beacon, 1968.

————. "The Problem of Identity, Selfhood and Image in New Nations." *Comparative Politics* 1, no. 3 (April 1969) pp. 297–312.

————. "The Fate of Human Rights in the Third World." *World Politics* 27, no. 2 (January 1975): pp. 201–226.

R. Emerson and M. Kilson, eds. *The Political Awakening of Africa.* Englewood Cliffs: Prentice Hall, 1965.

A. Enahoro. "Deux milles nations Africaines." *Jeune Afrique,* October 29, 1969.

H. Erlich. *The Struggle over Eritrea—War and Revolution in the Horn of Africa.* Stanford: Hoover Institution Press, 1983.

G. Espiell. *The Right of Self-Determination—Implementation of United Nations Resolutions.* New York: United Nations, 1980.

Ethiopia Observer, October 9, 1966.

W. Foltz. *From French West Africa to the Mali Federation.* New Haven: Yale University Press, 1965.

J. Forbes. "Do Tribes Have Rights—The Question of Self-Determination." *Journal of Human Relations* 28, no. 1 (1970): pp. 670–679.

C.J. Friedrich. *Man and His Government.* New York: McGraw-Hill, 1963.

J. Gerard-Libois. *Katanga Secession.* Madison: University of Wisconsin Press, 1966.

A.G. Gerteiny. "The Racial Factor and Politics in the Islamic Republic of Mauritania." *Race* 3, no. 1 (January 1967): pp. 263–275.

A.G.A.A. Ghaffar. *Politische Integration und Desintegration in einem Entwicklungsland—Dargestellt am Beispiel des Regionalen Konflikts in der Republik Sudan zwischen 1946–1969.* Frankfurt: Haag Herchen, 1979.

Ghana Today August 31, l960; June 20, 1962; March 10, 1965.

D. Gordon. *Self-Determination and History in the Third World.* Princeton: Princeton University Press, 1971.

A.J. Halbach. *Die Südafrikanischen Bantu Homelands—Konzeption, Struktur, Entwicklungsperspektiven.* München: Weltforum, 1976.

F. Halliday and M. Molyneux. *The Ethiopian Revolution.* London: Verso, 1981.

C. Hayes. *Historical Evolution of Modern Nationalism.* New York: Macmillan, 1948.

M. Hechter. *Internal Colonialism—The Celtic Fringe in British National Development 1536–1966.* London: Routledge and Kegan Paul, 1975.

F. Hertz. *Nationality in History and Politics—A Psychology and Sociology of National Sentiment and Nationalism.* London: Routledge and Kegan Paul, 1957.

A. Hirshman. "Exit, Voice and the State." *World Politics* 31, no. 1 (October 1978): pp. 90–107.

T. Hodges. *Western Sahara—The Roots of a Desert War.* Westport: Lawrence Hill, 1983.

T. Hodgkin. *Nationalism in Colonial Africa.* New York: New York University Press, 1965.

R. Jackson and C. Rosberg. "Why Africa's New States Persist: The Empirical and the Juridicial in Statehood." *World Politics* 35, no. 1 (October 1982): pp. 1–24.

O. Janowsky. *Nationalities and National Minorities.* New York: Macmillan, 1945.

I. Jennings. *An Approach to Self-Government.* Boston: Beacon 1963.

P.H. Judd. "The Attitudes of the African States toward the Katanga Secession—July 1960–January 1963." *Columbia Essays in International Affairs,* (1965): pp. 239–254.

O.S. Kamanu. "Secession and the Right of Self-Determination—An OAU Dilemma." *Journal of Modern African Studies* 12, no. 3 (1974): pp. 355–376.

T. Kanza. *Conflict in the Congo.* Harmondsworth: Penguin, 1972.

K. Kaunda. *A Humanist in Africa.* London: Longmans, 1969.

E. Kedourie. *Nationalism.* New York: Praeger, 1960.

————. *Nationalism in Asia and Africa*. New York: The World Publishing Company, 1970.

J. Kenyatta. "Pan African Nucleus." *Spearhead* 2, no. 2 (February 1962).

————. *Harambee—The Prime Minister of Kenya's Speeches 1963–1964*. Nairobi: Oxford University Press, 1964.

————. *Suffering Without Bitterness—The Founding of the Kenya Nation*. Nairobi: East African Publishing House, 1968.

A.H.M. Kirk-Greene, ed. *Crisis and Conflict in Nigeria—A Documentary Sourcebook 1966–1969*. Vols. I, II. London: Oxford University Press, 1971.

A.J. Klinghoffer. *The Angolan War—A Study in Soviet Policy in the Third World*. Boulder: Westview, 1980.

H. Kloss. *Grundfragen der Ethnopolitik im 20. Jahrhundert*. Bad Godesberg: Wissenschaftliches Archiv, 1969.

H. Kohn. *Nationalism—Its Meaning and History*. New York: Van Nostrand, 1965.

————. *The Idea of Nationalism—A Study in its Origins and Background*. New York: Collier, 1967.

R. Léfort. *Ethiopia—An Heretical Revolution*. London: Zed Press, 1983.

C. Legum. "Somali Liberation Songs." *Journal of Modern African Studies* 1, no. 4 (1963): 503–519.

————. *Pan Africanism—A Short Political Guide*. New York: Praeger, 1965.

R. Lemarchand. "The Bases of Nationalism among the Bakongo." *Africa*, no. 4 (Winter 1961): pp. 344–354.

————. *Rwanda and Burundi*. New York: Praeger, 1970.

E. Lemberg. *Nationalismus—Psychologie und Geschichte*. Hamburg: Rowohlt, 1964.

V.I. Lenin. *Selected Works*. Vols. 2, 4. Moscow: Cooperative Publishing Society for Foreign Workers in the USSR, 1935.

————. *Collected Works*. Vol. 10. New York: International Publishers, 1938.

————. *The Right of Nations to Self-Determination*. New York: International Publishers, 1951.

V. Levine. "The Politics of Partition in Africa." *Journal of International Affairs* 18, no. 2 (1964): pp. 198–210.

————. *The Cameroun Federal Republic*. Ithaca: Cornell University Press, 1971.

I.M. Lewis. *The Modern History of Somaliland—From Nation to State*. New York: Praeger, 1965.

————. ed. *Nationalism and Self-Determination in the Horn of Africa*. London: Ithaca Press, 1983.

A. Lijphart. *Democracy in Plural Societies—A Comparative Exploration*. New Haven: Yale University Press, 1977.

E. Lofoli. "Le Principe de l'autodetermination des peuples et des nations et son application en Afrique." *Etudes Congolaises* 12, no. 3 (July-September 1969).

C.A. MaCartney. *National States and National Minorities*. London: Oxford University Press, 1934.

B. Malwal. *People and Power in the Sudan—The Struggle for National Stability*. London: Ithaca Press, 1984.

M.W. Mariam. "The Background of the Ethio-Somalian Dispute." *Journal of Modern African Studies* 2, no. 2 (1964): pp. 189–219.

V. Matthies. *Der Grenzkonflikt Somalias mit Äthiopien und Kenya*. Hamburg: Institut fur Afrikakunde, 1977.

————. *Der Eritrea Konflikt—Ein Vergessener Kreig am Horn Afrika*. Hamburg: Institut fur Afrikakunde, 1981.

A. Mazrui. "On the Concept 'We are all Africans.'" *American Political Science Review* 57, no. 1 (March 1963): pp. 88–97.

————. *Towards a Pax Africana—A Study in Ideology and Ambition.* London: Weidenfeld and Nicolson, 1967.

————. *On Heroes and Uhuru Worship.* London: Longmans, 1967.

A. Mazrui and M. Tidy. *Nationalism and New States in Africa.* Nairobi: Heinemann, 1984.

T. Mboya. *Freedom and After.* Boston: Little Brown, 1963.

————. *Challenge of Nationhood.* London: Heinemann, 1970.

M.C. McEwen. *International Boundaries in East Africa.* Oxford: The Clarendon Press, 1970.

F. Meinecke. *Weltbürgertum und Nationalstaat.* München: Oldenburg, 1928.

J.S. Mill. *On Representative Government.* Indianapolis: Library of Liberal Arts Press, 1958.

L. Miller. *World Order and Local Disorder—The United Nations and Internal Conflict.* Princeton: Princeton University Press, 1967.

K. Minogue. *Nationalism.* London: Batsford, 1967.

E. Mortimer. *France and the Africans 1944–1960—A Political History.* New York: Walker and Company, 1969.

D. Mudola. "The Search for the Nation-State and African Peace." *East Africa Journal* 6, no. 2 (November 1969): pp. 17–22.

D.C. Mulford. *Zambia—The Politics of Independence 1957–1964.* Oxford: Oxford University Press, 1967.

G.C.M. Mutiso and S.W. Rohio, eds. *Readings in African Political Thought.* London: Oxford University Press, 1975.

Nationalism—A Report by a Study Group of the Royal Institute of International Affairs. New York: Kelley, 1966.

The Nationalist (Dar es Salaam), April 14, 1968; April 27, 1968; May 3, 1968; May 21, 1968.

B. Neuberger. "What is a Nation?—A Contribution to the Debate on the Palestinian Question." *State, Government and International Relations.* (Hebrew University), no. 9 (May 1976): pp. 90–108. (Hebrew).

————. "The African Concept of Balkanization." *Journal of Modern African Studies* 13, no. 3 (1976): pp. 523–529.

————. "State and Nation in African Thought." *Journal of African Studies* 4, no. 2 (1977): pp. 198–205.

————. *The Ethnic Problem in Africa and the Wars of Katanga and Biafra.* Tel Aviv: Israeli Open University, 1979. (Hebrew).

————. *Involvement, Invasion and Withdrawal—Qaddafi's Libya and Chad 1969–1981.* Tel Aviv: Shiloah Center for Middle Eastern and African Studies, 1982.

M. Newitt. *The Comoro Islands—Struggle Against Dependency in the Indian Ocean.* Boulder: Westview, 1984.

New York Times, January 19, 1971.

R. Nixon. "Self-Determination: The Nigeria-Biafra Case." *World Politics* 24, no. 4 (July 1972): pp. 473–497.

K. Nkrumah. *Ghana—The Autobiography of Kwame Nkrumah.* New York: Nelson and Sons, 1957.

————. *I Speak for Freedom.* New York: Praeger, 1961.

————. *Handbook for Revolutionary Warfare.* London: Panaf Books, 1968.

————. *Dark Days in Ghana.* New York: International Publishers, 1969.

————. *Class Struggle in Africa.* New York: International Publishers, 1970.

E. Nordlinger. *Conflict Regulation in Divided Societies.* Cambridge: Center for International Affairs, Harvard University, 1972.

G.A. Nweke. *External Intervention in African Conflicts: France and French Speaking*

Africa in the Nigerian Civil War. Boston: African Studies Center, Boston University, 1976.

J. Nyerere. "Tanganyika Today—A Nationalist View." *International Affairs* 36, no. 1 (January 1960): pp. 43–47.

———. "A United States for Africa." *Journal of Modern African Studies* 1, no. 1 (Spring 1963): pp. 1–6.

———. *Freedom and Unity—Uhuru na Umoja.* Dar es Salaam: Oxford University Press, 1966.

———. "Why We Recognized Biafra." *The Observer,* April 28, 1968.

R.F. Nyrop et al. *Area Handbook for Rwanda.* Washington: U.S. Government, 1969.

C.C. O'Brien. *To Katanga and Back.* London: Hutchinson, 1962.

———. "The Right to Secede." *New York Times,* December 30, 1971.

J. Oduho and W. Deng. *The Problem of the Southern Sudan.* London: Oxford University Press, 1963.

W. Ofuatey-Kodjoe. *The Principle of Self-Determination in International Law.* New York: Nellen, 1977.

O. Ojukwu. *Biafra I—Selected Speeches with Journal of Events.* New York: Harper and Row, 1969.

———. *Biafra II—Random Thoughts.* New York: Harper and Row, 1969.

J. Okello. *Revolution in Zanzibar.* Nairobi: East African Publishing House, 1967.

V. Oluronsola, ed. *The Politics of Cultural Subnationalism in Africa.* Garden City: Doubleday, 1972.

J. Ostheimer. *The Politics of Western Indian Ocean Islands.* New York: Praeger, 1975.

T. Otegbeye. "Nigeria and the National Question." *World Marxist Review* 12, no. 10 (October 1969): pp. 48–52.

J. Paden, ed. *Values, Identities and National Integration—Empirical Research in Africa.* Evanston: Northwestern University Press, 1980.

J. Plamenatz. *On Alien Rule and Self-Government.* London: Longmans, 1960.

M. Pomerance. *Self-Determination in Law and Practice.* The Hauge: M. Nijhoff, 1982.

K. Rabl. *Das Selbstbestimmungsrecht der Völker—Geschichtliche Grundlagen und Umriss der gegenwärtigen Bedeutung.* Köln: Bohlau Verlag, 1973.

J.E. Reece. "Internal Colonialism: The Case of Brittany." *Ethnic and Racial Studies* 2, no. 3 (July 1979): pp. 275–292.

M. Reisman and B.H. Weston, eds. *Toward World Order and Human Dignity.* New York: The Free Press, 1976.

E. Rénan. *Qu'est-ce qu'une nation?* Paris: Calman Levy, 1882.

D. Ronen. *The Quest for Self-Determination.* New Haven: Yale University Press, 1979.

C. Rosberg. "National Identity in African States." *The African Review* 1, no. 1 (March 1971): 79–92.

R. Rotberg. "African Nationalism: Concept or Confusion." *Journal of Modern African Studies* 4, no. 1 (1966): pp. 33–46.

D. Rothchild. *The Politics of Integration—An East African Documentary.* Nairobi: East African Publishing House, 1968.

———. "The Two Senses of Ethno-national Self-Determination." *Africa Report* 26, no. 11–12 (1981): pp. 56–58.

D. Rothchild and V. Oluronsola, eds. *State Versus Ethnic Claims: African Policy Dilemmas.* Boulder: Westview Press, 1983.

J. Rothschild. *Ethnopolitics—A Conceptual Framework.* New York: Columbia University Press, 1981.

D. Rustow. *A World of Nations—Problems of Political Modernization.* Washington: The Brookings Institution, 1967.

J.N. Saxena. *Self-Determination from Biafra to Bangladesh.* Delhi: University of

Delhi, 1978.
B.H. Selassie. *Conflict and Intervention in the Horn of Africa.* New York: Monthly Review Press, 1980.
L. Senghor. *On African Socialism.* New York: Praeger, 1964.
B. Shafer. *Nationalism—Myth and Reality.* London: Gollancz, 1955.
A.J. Shelton. "The Black Mystique—Reactionary Extremes in 'Negritude.'" *African Affairs* 63, no. 25 (April 1964): pp. 115–127.
F.L. Shiels, ed. *Ethnic Separatism and World Politics.* Lanham: University Press of America, 1984.
Somali Republic and African Unity. (Nairobi, 1962).
A.D. Smith. *Theories of Nationalism.* New York: Harper and Row, 1971.
———. *Nationalism in the Twentieth Century.* Oxford: Robertson, 1979.
———. *The Ethnic Revival in the Modern World.* Cambridge: Cambridge University Press, 1981.
A.D. Smith, ed. *Nationalist Movements.* London: Macmillan Press, 1976.
J. Stone. "Introduction: Internal Colonialism in Comparative Perspective." *Ethnic and Racial Studies* 2, no. 3 (July 1979): pp. 255–56.
J. Stremlau. *The International Politics of the Nigerian Civil War 1967–1970.* Princeton: Princeton University Press, 1977.
N. Stultz. *Transkei's Half Loaf.* New Haven: Yale University Press, 1979.
A.R. Sureda. *The Evolution of the Right of Self-Determination: A Study of United Nations Practice.* Leiden: A.W. Sijthoff, 1973.
T.N. Tamuno. "Separatist Agitation in Nigeria since 1914." *Journal of Modern African Studies,* (1970): pp. 563–584.
R. Tholomier. *Djibouti—Pawn in the Horn of Africa.* Metuchen: Scarecrow Press, 1981.
S. Touré. *L'Afrique et la révolution.* Paris: Présence Africaine, n.d.
———. *Doctrine and Methods of the Democratic Party of Guinea.* N.p., n.d.
———. *Guinean Revolution and Social Progress.* Cairo: Societé Orientale de Publicité, n.d.
S. Touval. "The Organization of African Unity and African Borders." *International Organisation* 21, no. 1 (1967): pp. 101–127.
———. *Boundary Politics in Africa.* Cambridge: Harvard University Press, 1972.
H.V. Treitschke. *Politics.* New York: Harcourt, Brace and World Company, 1968.
P. Tsiranana. "Madagaskars Weg Zur Unabhängigkeit." *Afrika Heute* II (1960): pp. 29–33.
J. Tubiana, ed. *Modern Ethiopia—From Accession of Menelik to the Present.* Rotterdam: Balkema, 1980.
Uganda Argus (Kampala), February 3, 1960.
U.O. Umozurike. *Self-Determination in International Law.* N.p.: Archon Books, 1972.
D. Wai. "Sources of Communal Conflict and Secessionist Policies in Africa." *Ethnic and Racial Studies* 1, no. 3 (July 1978): pp. 281–305.
I. Wallerstein. *Africa—The Politics of Unity.* New York: Random House, 1961.
M. Walzer. *Just and Unjust Wars—A Moral Argument with Historical Illustrations.* New York: Basic Books, 1977.
S. Wambaugh. *Plebiscites since the World War.* Washington: Carnegie Endowment for International Peace, 1933.
Washington Post, March 8, 1967.
R. Weisfelder. "The Basotho Nation-State—What Legacy for the Future." *Journal of Modern African Studies* 19, no. 2 (1981): pp. 221–256.
C. Welch. *Dream of Unity—Pan Africanism and Political Integration in West Africa.* Ithaca: Cornell University Press, 1966.

West Africa, September 16, 1961, May 10, 1968, October 5, 1968, August 15, 1970.

C.G. Widstrand, ed. *African Boundary Problems.* Stockholm: Almquist and Widsell, 1969.

H.A. Winkler, ed. *Nationalismus in der Welt von heute.* Göttingen: Vandenhoeck und Ruprecht, 1982.

L.W. Wiseberg. "Human Rights in Africa—Towards a Definition of the Problem of a Double Standard." *Issue* 6, no. 4 (Winter 1976): pp. 3–13.

C. Young. *Politics in the Congo—Decolonization and Independence.* Princeton: Princeton University Press, 1965.

——— . *The Politics of Cultural Pluralism.* Madison: The University of Wisconsin Press, 1976.